CUSTOMERS' COOKBOOK

A Collection of Favorite Recipes

Recipes developed by Miriam B. Loo
and her Test Kitchen Staff

Test Kitchen Supervisor — Pat Morrison
Photographer — Ron Oatney
Food Stylist — Marjorie Read Moureau

Born and raised in Topeka, Kansas, MIRIAM BAKER LOO is an accomplished businesswoman and creative homemaker who has been an enthusiastic cook since her youth. After her graduation from Washburn University of Topeka, from which she recently received the Outstanding Achievement Award, she married Orin Loo, an artist and lithographer. The Loo family later moved to Colorado Springs, Colorado, where in 1950, with the help of her husband, Miriam founded Current, Inc.

Current® is a national mail order firm which has grown from a basement business in the Loo home, when the product line included Post-A-Note® cards and recipe cards designed by Mr. Loo, to a thriving enterprise serving millions of customers.

Miriam Loo introduced recipes into the Current line by including them on note cards and calendars, and now the company publishes several cookbooks each year. In 1979, she established the Current Test Kitchen, which today includes four kitchens and a staff of six home economists who carefully test each Current recipe. She attends gourmet cooking classes and makes public appearances on behalf of Current all over the country, yet she still enjoys cooking and entertaining for her family (including three grown sons and five grandchildren) and friends.

Long involved in volunteer activities, Miriam Loo has received national recognition for her accomplishments in community work, church leadership and business.

Pictured on the cover, top to bottom, are Bacon-Onion Oatmeal Buns (see page 19), Savory Picnic Snak Bread (see page 22), and Honey-Oatmeal White Bread (see page 20).

Dear Friends,

Your response to my request for recipes some time ago was overwhelming! More than ten thousand recipes of all kinds came in, many with heartwarming letters and personal notes.

The result was this wonderful cookbook consisting entirely of recipes from you! You can imagine how difficult it was to select just over one hundred recipes for publication. First, my Test Kitchen Staff sorted all the recipes into categories. Believe me, they were surrounded with boxes. Then duplicate recipes were screened out since originality was one of the qualities we were looking for. This still left thousands of recipes to read and select from. We finally picked about two hundred and fifty different dishes to test that represented all the categories. Then the fun began.

For months we sampled recipes from all over the country and from foreign lands where some of our customers are living. At the tasting sessions, the tester would read the recipe and whatever comments or history went along with it. Some folks even sent pictures of themselves and their families, so we felt we really got to know them personally. The final selection process was really a matter of picking the very best recipes that gave the most variety and originality to the book. Many good recipes had to be eliminated because we felt they were too similar to something we had already chosen.

I can hardly express my thanks to all of you who happily submitted not only your recipes but your friendly good wishes and interesting stories. If your recipe doesn't appear in this book, it's because we simply didn't have space for the many outstanding entries we received.

I know you will all enjoy this sharing of recipes almost as much as I did.

Sincerely,

Miriam B. Loo

TABLE OF CONTENTS

Potpourri

HEARTY OXTAIL SOUP

"My recipe had never been written down. I've been married 52 years and have made the soup many times, just from memory. Since then I've written it down for my daughter-in-law. Once when making the soup with my granddaughter who was 9 years old, she asked, 'Grandma, are those really ox tails?' I said, 'Yes, they really are.' She then said, 'If I was an ox, I would always be sitting down.' "

2 pounds beef oxtails, trimmed	¾ cup cut green beans
¾ cup chopped onion	¾ cup chopped cabbage
2 teaspoons beef bouillon granules	½ cup shredded carrot
2 teaspoons salt	½ cup chopped celery
¾ teaspoon pepper	1 small bay leaf
1 to 1½ cups noodles, broken	2 tablespoons chopped parsley
1 can (16 oz.) whole tomatoes, chopped	1½ teaspoons sugar
1 can (6 oz.) tomato paste	½ to 1 teaspoon dried thyme leaves, crushed
	½ to 1 teaspoon dried marjoram leaves, crushed

In an 8-quart saucepot, place oxtails. Cover with 3 inches of water. Add onion, bouillon granules, salt and pepper. Over high heat, bring to a boil; reduce heat to low, cover and simmer for 3 to 4 hours or until meat is very tender. Skim off fat.

Add noodles, tomatoes with juice, tomato paste, green beans, cabbage, carrot, celery, bay leaf, parsley, sugar, thyme and marjoram. Over high heat, bring to a boil; reduce heat to low, cover and simmer for 45 minutes or until vegetables are tender. Makes 8 to 10 hearty servings.

Mrs. W. W. O'Brien
Glen Ellyn, IL

Mrs. W. W. O'Brien

Pictured on the preceding page, top to bottom, are Coquito (see page 11), Apricot Mist Punch (see page 14), Shrimp Butter (see page 10), Chutney-Stuffed Eggs (see page 13), and Green Chili Cheese Snacks (see page 14).

ICED TEA FOR A CROWD

"This is a very simple recipe, but I've had so many people enjoy it and remember how good it tasted. That's why I thought of sharing it with you. It's a favorite in our house all year round, and I never make less than a gallon because it goes so fast. We use this more than soda."

3 quarts water	1 can (12 oz.) pink lemonade
¾ cup sugar	concentrate
8 tea bags	

In a large saucepan over medium heat, bring water to a boil. Remove from heat. Stir in sugar until dissolved. Add tea bags. Steep for 5 minutes or until desired strength. Remove tea bags. Cool. Add lemonade concentrate and enough additional water to equal 1 gallon total liquid. Store in a gallon jar. Stir before serving over ice. Makes 1 gallon.

Joan Schauer
Islip Terrace, NY

PIZZA APPETIZERS

"What makes this recipe so nice is that the spread can be made a day or two ahead and stored in the refrigerator. Takes only a few minutes to assemble and 2 to 3 minutes to broil. Terrific for the busy host or hostess. They are the hit of a party and the men love them."

1 pound bulk Italian sausage, crumbled	⅛ teaspoon ground oregano
	Dash of garlic powder
1 package (4 oz.) shredded sharp Cheddar cheese	Dash of salt
	Dash of pepper
1 package (4 oz.) shredded mozzarella cheese	⅔ cup mayonnaise
	48 slices cocktail rye bread

In a 10-inch skillet over medium heat, brown sausage. Drain off fat. Cool meat.
In a medium bowl, stir sausage, cheeses, oregano, garlic powder, salt and pepper. Stir in mayonnaise until mixture is well moistened and holds together. Add more mayonnaise if needed. Cover and refrigerate until ready to use.
To serve, preheat broiler. Spread about 1 tablespoon of the mixture on each slice of bread. Broil 6 inches from heat source for 2 minutes or until bubbly. Makes 48.

Lorraine Lubenkov
Berwyn, IL

CHUCK'S TERIYAKI SAUCE

"I prefer to use this marinade on sirloin steaks and serve them with rice and sautéed mushrooms."

- 1 cup soy sauce
- ½ cup water
- ¼ cup packed brown sugar
- ¼ cup whiskey
- 2 teaspoons ground ginger
- 2 teaspoons onion salt
- 2 teaspoons Worcestershire sauce
- 1 large clove garlic, minced

In a small bowl, stir soy sauce, water, brown sugar, whiskey, ginger, onion salt, Worcestershire sauce and garlic until brown sugar is dissolved.

Place mixture in a plastic bag; add meat, poultry or shrimp and marinate for 2 to 6 hours in the refrigerator. Drain marinade and cook meat as desired. Makes 2 cups.

Charles E. Henderson
Beverly, MA

PEPPY PORK SOUP

"My mother used to make a similar soup using dry Great Northern beans. During the Depression, I remember a neighbor had extra beans to harvest and he loaned us a team of horses and a wagon to harvest them. Our family of nine children all pitched in and shelled the beans. We ate lots of bean soup that winter!"

- 1½ cups dry small white navy beans
- ¾ pound cubed lean pork
- 2 tablespoons vegetable oil
- ½ cup chopped onion
- 1 large clove garlic, minced
- ¾ to 1 teaspoon chili powder
- ½ teaspoon ground cumin
- ½ teaspoon dried oregano leaves, crushed
- 8 cups water
- 2 tablespoons chicken bouillon granules
- 1 can (4 oz.) whole green chilies, drained and chopped

Rinse beans and place in a large bowl; cover with water. Soak overnight.

In a heavy 5-quart Dutch oven over medium heat, sauté pork in oil until it loses its pink color. Remove meat and set aside. In Dutch oven, sauté onion and garlic for 3 minutes or until golden. Return meat to Dutch oven. Add chili powder, cumin and oregano. Drain beans and add to meat mixture. Add 8 cups water and bouillon granules. Over high heat, bring to a boil; reduce heat to low, cover and simmer for 1½ hours. Add green chilies and simmer 30 minutes longer or until beans are tender. Makes 10 (1-cup) servings.

Helen G. Wasson
Hagerman, ID

SAUSAGE SOUP

"I enjoy cooking for large family gatherings — mostly just plain, old-fashioned cooking. I have a large garden and enjoy taking care of it."

2 pounds sweet Italian sausage, casings removed and crumbled
2 cups finely chopped onions
2 cloves garlic, minced
1 can (16 oz.) whole tomatoes
4 cups water
2 cans (10½ oz. each) condensed beef broth
1 cup red wine
⅓ cup minced parsley
1 teaspoon dried basil leaves, crushed
½ teaspoon dried thyme leaves, crushed
2 large zucchini, thinly sliced (about 4 cups)
1 cup uncooked small pasta shells
1 small green pepper, finely chopped
Grated Parmesan cheese
Hot Italian bread

In a 5-quart Dutch oven over medium heat, brown sausage; drain off fat. Add onions and garlic. Sauté for 5 minutes or until onions are limp. Stir in and break up tomatoes. Add water, beef broth, wine, parsley, basil and thyme. Bring to a boil; reduce heat to low, cover and simmer for 25 to 30 minutes.

Add zucchini, pasta and green pepper. Over medium heat, bring to a boil; reduce heat to low, cover and simmer for 25 minutes or until vegetables and pasta are done.

Serve in soup bowls and sprinkle with cheese. Serve with Italian bread. Makes 8 to 10 servings.

Mrs. Atrell Winn
Fremont, CA

HONEY CHICKEN WINGS

"They're gooey and simply delicious!"

16 chicken wings (about 3 lb.)	2 teaspoons vegetable oil
1 cup honey	2 large cloves garlic, crushed
½ cup catsup	and minced
½ cup soy sauce	Pepper (optional)

Preheat oven to 375°. Cut off bony tips of wings (reserve for another use). Cut each wing in half at the joint. Place in a single layer in a shallow 3-quart baking dish. In a medium bowl, stir honey, catsup, soy sauce, oil, garlic and pepper until well blended. Pour over chicken pieces, turning to coat. Bake for 1¼ to 1½ hours or until browned, basting occasionally.

To serve, transfer to a chafing dish or hot tray. Serve with small plates and napkins. Makes 32 appetizers.

Susan K. Gray
Warminster, PA

SHRIMP BUTTER

(pictured on page 5)

"I serve this in a small lotus bowl or mold a shape on a bed of lettuce with crackers as an hors d'oeuvre. Most people who taste Shrimp Butter request the recipe."

1 package (3 oz.) cream cheese, softened	1 teaspoon minced onion
6 tablespoons butter, softened	1 can (4½ oz.) tiny cocktail shrimp,* rinsed and well drained (reserve several for garnish)
2 tablespoons mayonnaise	
1 tablespoon lemon juice	

In a small mixer bowl at medium speed, beat cream cheese and butter until fluffy. Add mayonnaise, lemon juice and onion; beat until well blended. Add shrimp and beat at low speed just until mixed. Spoon into serving dish. Garnish with reserved shrimp. Cover and refrigerate at least 2 hours or until firm. Makes 1⅓ cups.

*Crabmeat may be substituted.

Jeanie Spierdowis
Newburgh, IN

COQUITO (Spanish-Style Eggnog)

(pictured on page 5)

"I serve this in place of the traditional eggnog during the holidays. I learned basic cooking techniques by assisting friends in their restaurant and catering business, then added experience with other people of various ethnic backgrounds through travel and career when ideas and techniques were shared."

1 cup sugar	1½ to 2 cups light rum
4 eggs	½ teaspoon vanilla extract
1 can (15 oz.) cream of coconut	Ground nutmeg
1 can (13 oz.) evaporated milk or 1¾ cups whipping cream	

In a large mixer bowl at medium speed, beat sugar and eggs for 2 minutes or until thick and creamy. Add cream of coconut, evaporated milk or cream, rum and vanilla. Beat at low speed until well blended. Pour into a large glass jar; cover and chill at least 1 hour. Shake or stir before serving. Sprinkle with nutmeg. Best served the same day. Makes about 12 (4-ounce) servings.

Susan Kamer-Shinaberry
Charleston, WV

GOLDIE'S POPCORN PARTY MIX

"This is a yummy snack — a little different — that's always a hit! Serve in a large decorative bowl for parties."

3 quarts popped corn, unsalted	½ cup butter or margarine, melted
4 cups bite-size crispy rice cereal squares	⅓ cup packed brown sugar
1 cup coarsely chopped walnuts or mixed nuts	1 package (1.25 oz.) taco seasoning mix

Preheat oven to 300°. In a large bowl, mix popped corn, rice cereal and nuts. Pour butter or margarine over mixture; stir to coat.

In a small bowl, stir brown sugar and taco seasoning until blended. Sprinkle over corn mixture; toss to mix well. Spread evenly in two 15½ × 10½ × 1-inch jelly roll pans. Bake for 5 minutes; stir. Bake 3 to 5 minutes longer or until brown sugar is melted and mixture is heated through. Makes 16 cups.

Lily M. Butler
Federal Way, WA

SHRIMP BISQUE

"This is a delicious luncheon appetizer soup served with thinly sliced turkey; buttered party rye bread; salad of greens, grapefruit sections, avocado, onion, fresh mushrooms and a vinaigrette dressing; fruit compote and pound cake."

½ cup chopped onion
2 tablespoons butter
2 cans (10¾ oz. each) condensed cream of celery
   soup
2 cups half-and-half
¼ pound mushrooms, sliced
1 soup can milk (1¼ cups)
3 cans (6½ oz. each) minced
   clams, drained and ¾ cup
   liquid reserved
¼ cup diced pimiento

2 tablespoons dry sherry
1 tablespoon chopped
   parsley
1 tablespoon Worcestershire
   sauce
¼ teaspoon paprika
¼ teaspoon white pepper
1 pound cooked shrimp, cut
   in half if large
Crushed saltine crackers or
   instant potato flakes
   (optional)

In a heavy 2-quart saucepan over medium heat, sauté onion in butter for 3 to 5 minutes or until transparent. Add cream of celery soup, half-and-half, mushrooms, milk, reserved clam liquid, pimiento, sherry, parsley, Worcestershire sauce, paprika and white pepper. Bring to a boil; reduce heat to low and simmer, uncovered, for 30 minutes, stirring occasionally.

Add shrimp and clams. Heat through (do not boil). Thin with additional clam liquid or thicken with crackers or potato flakes. Serve immediately. To reheat leftovers, use a double boiler. Makes 14 (½-cup) servings.

Mrs. George Brumley
Sea Island, GA

HOLIDAY SPICE BOWL

"Creates a pleasant, heavenly smell throughout the home during the Thanksgiving and Christmas holidays. This recipe was handed down from my grandmother." (Note: This is not to be consumed.)

1 orange
1 lemon
2 large bay leaves

1 cinnamon stick (3 inches
   long)
2 tablespoons whole cloves

Fill a heavy 5-quart Dutch oven or a heavy 3-quart saucepan half full of hot water. Peel orange and lemon; reserve fruit for another use. Place orange and lemon peels, bay leaves, cinnamon stick and cloves in water. Over high heat, bring to a boil; reduce heat to low and simmer uncovered or partially covered. Add more water if needed. Store covered in refrigerator. Reheat as desired.

Robin L. Cozzolino
Saginaw, MI

CHUTNEY-STUFFED EGGS

(pictured on page 5)

6 large hard-cooked eggs	1 teaspoon curry powder
2 to 3 tablespoons mayonnaise	⅛ teaspoon celery salt
2 tablespoons butter, softened	⅛ teaspoon onion salt
	2 tablespoons chutney

Cut eggs in half lengthwise. Remove yolks from eggs and place in a medium bowl; set whites aside. Mash yolks with a fork. Add mayonnaise, butter, curry powder, celery salt and onion salt; mix until smooth. Using a decorating bag fitted with a star tube, fill each egg white with egg yolk mixture, piping around edge to form a rim. Place a scant ½ teaspoon chutney in center of each. Chill for 1 to 2 hours before serving. Makes 12.

Edythe D. Perdue
Columbus, OH

VEGETABLE CHOWDER

"This particular recipe was created through a mishap of sorts. Our freezer went out one long holiday weekend, and even though we attempted to keep everything ice-packed, some of my vegetables began to thaw. So I began to use my imagination and was able to create this delicious soup out of sheer necessity."

2 cans (14½ oz. each) clear chicken broth	2 tablespoons butter or margarine
1 package (10 oz.) frozen chopped broccoli	¼ cup all-purpose flour
1 package (10 oz.) frozen cauliflower	½ teaspoon salt
3 slices bacon, cut in ½-inch pieces	⅛ teaspoon pepper
1 cup chopped onion	2½ cups milk
	1 can (17 oz.) cream-style corn

In a 4-quart saucepot over high heat, bring chicken broth, broccoli and cauliflower to a boil. Reduce heat to low, cover and simmer for 10 minutes or until vegetables are tender.

Meanwhile, in a 10-inch skillet over medium heat, fry bacon until almost crisp. Add onion and sauté for 5 minutes or until onion is transparent. Add butter or margarine. Stir until melted. Stir in flour, salt and pepper. Cook and stir for 1 to 2 minutes. Add milk. Stirring, bring to a boil and boil until thickened. Stir into broccoli-cauliflower mixture. Add corn. Cook over low heat for 15 minutes to blend flavors, stirring occasionally. Makes 8 (about 1⅓-cup) servings.

Joan M. Pfeifer
Rockford, IL

GREEN CHILI CHEESE SNACKS

(pictured on page 5)

"An easy-to-make recipe for unexpected guests. They're delicious served with guacamole dip."

¾ cup shredded sharp Cheddar cheese
1 package (3 oz.) cream cheese, softened
3 tablespoons chopped green chilies

1 teaspoon onion powder
1 can (8 oz.) refrigerated crescent dinner rolls
Sliced jalapeño or bell peppers (optional)

Preheat oven to 425°. Generously grease a baking sheet or use a non-stick baking sheet. In a medium bowl, combine Cheddar cheese, cream cheese, green chilies and onion powder; set aside. Separate dinner rolls into four rectangles. On waxed paper, roll each piece into an 8×6-inch rectangle; pinch perforations together. Spread a scant ¼ cup of the cheese mixture on each rectangle. Starting from short side, roll as for a jelly roll. Chill in freezer for 10 minutes. With a sharp knife slice each roll into ten pieces. Place cut-side down on baking sheet. Bake for 8 to 10 minutes or until golden. If desired, garnish with peppers. Serve warm. Makes 40.

Nanci Curley
Albuquerque, NM

APRICOT MIST PUNCH

(pictured on page 5)

"This is a non-alcoholic punch for parties and showers that is refreshing without being too sweet. I have found that men really like this punch also. I often make an ice ring using the punch ingredients with strawberries and thin slices of lime floating in it."

1 can (46 oz.) apricot or peach nectar, chilled
1 can (46 oz.) unsweetened pineapple juice, chilled
3 cans (6 oz. each) frozen limeade concentrate, thawed

3 bottles (28 oz. each) ginger ale, chilled
Ice cubes or ice ring

Pour nectar, pineapple juice and limeade concentrate into a large punch bowl. Pour ginger ale down side of punch bowl. Stir gently to mix. Add ice. Makes 38 (5-ounce) servings.

Teresa Cudzewicz
Sugar Grove, IL

Breads

GLAZED APPLE COFFEE CROWN

"I serve this at brunches and buffets. Also at Thanksgiving. The light texture and taste is like that of cinnamon rolls."

4½ to 5 cups all-purpose flour	¾ cup sugar
⅓ cup sugar	1 package (3 oz.) cream
1 package active dry yeast	cheese, softened
1 teaspoon salt	1½ teaspoons ground
1 cup milk	cinnamon
½ cup water	2 cups peeled, chopped tart
½ cup butter or margarine,	apples
softened	⅓ cup packed brown sugar
1 egg	Lemon Glaze (see next page)

In a large bowl, combine 2 cups of the flour, ⅓ cup sugar, yeast and salt; set aside.

In a small saucepan over medium heat, heat milk, water and ¼ cup of the butter or margarine until warm (120° to 130°). Pour over flour mixture; add egg and beat by hand for 2 minutes. Stir in 2 cups of the flour until blended. On a lightly floured surface, knead for about 5 minutes or until smooth and elastic, adding additional flour as needed to prevent sticking. Place in a greased bowl; turn to coat surface. Cover and let rise in a warm place, free from drafts, until doubled, about 1 hour.

Grease two 9 × 1½-inch round cake pans. In a small mixer bowl at low speed, beat ¾ cup sugar, cream cheese, remaining ¼ cup butter or margarine, and 1 teaspoon of the cinnamon until smooth; set aside.

In a small bowl, mix apples, brown sugar and remaining ½ teaspoon cinnamon; set aside.

Divide dough into two portions. On a lightly floured surface, roll one portion into an 18 × 8-inch rectangle. Spread half of the cream cheese mixture to within ½ inch of edge. Cover with half of the apple mixture. Starting from the long side, roll tightly as for a jelly roll. Pinch edges and ends to seal. Form into a ring and place seam-side down in a cake pan. Repeat with remaining dough and fillings. Cover and let rise in a warm place, free from drafts, until doubled, about 45 minutes. With a skewer, gently pierce each ring halfway down in several places. Bake in a preheated 350° oven on lowest rack for 40 minutes. Cover top loosely with foil and bake 15 minutes longer or until medium brown. Remove from pan. Pour glaze over warm coffee cake and serve. Makes 2.

continued on next page . . .

Pictured on the preceding page, top to bottom, are Bacon-Onion Oatmeal Buns (see page 19), Savory Picnic Snak Bread (see page 22), and Honey-Oatmeal White Bread (see page 20).

Glazed Apple Coffee Crown continued . . .

LEMON GLAZE

1 cup powdered sugar	2 tablespoons milk
2 tablespoons butter or margarine, softened	1 teaspoon lemon juice

In a small bowl, stir powdered sugar, butter or margarine, milk and lemon juice until smooth. Pour over warm Apple Coffee Crown or coffee cake of your choice. Makes ½ cup.

Leslie Coppedge
Miami, OK

VICTORIA'S BANANA BREAD

"The very ripe bananas are the flavor secret in this moist, sweet bread. Serve it plain or with softened butter or cream cheese for dessert or with coffee anytime."

2 cups very ripe mashed bananas (about 4 to 5 medium)	1 teaspoon baking soda
	¼ teaspoon salt
½ cup sugar	1½ cups ground almonds
1 egg	½ cup raisins
1 teaspoon vanilla extract	½ cup unprocessed bran flakes*
1½ cups whole wheat flour	
1 teaspoon baking powder	⅓ cup butter, melted

Preheat oven to 350°. Grease a 9 × 5 × 3-inch loaf pan. Line with waxed paper; grease and flour waxed paper. In a large bowl, beat bananas, sugar, egg and vanilla until well blended. Stir in whole wheat flour, baking powder, baking soda and salt until well mixed. Stir in almonds, raisins, bran flakes and butter until blended and bran is moistened. Pour into pan. Bake for 1 hour or until a wooden pick inserted in center comes out clean. Remove from pan, peel off waxed paper and cool on a wire rack.

Wrap and store in the refrigerator at least one day or up to two weeks. Makes 1 loaf.

*Unprocessed bran flakes can be obtained in the health food section of supermarkets or in health food stores.

Victoria Angelini
Newport Beach, CA

GRANDMA'S DUMPLEDORFS

"This original recipe is from my husband's grandmother, who came to Kremmling by buckboard before the turn of the century. She married a rancher, and we now own the same ranch. When her family was tired of potatoes or rice along with the ever-present beef, she made dumplings — great big ones! Our children simply gobbled them up, calling them 'Grandma's Dumpledorfs'. Beef gravy was originally used instead of the soup which is my idea."

1 can (10¾ oz.) condensed cream of celery soup*	Milk (about ¾ cup)
1 soup can water (1¼ cups)	1½ cups all-purpose flour
2 tablespoons butter or margarine	1¼ teaspoons baking powder
1 large egg	1 teaspoon dried parsley flakes (optional)
	½ teaspoon salt

In a 5-quart Dutch oven or heavy saucepot over medium heat, stir soup, water and butter or margarine until smooth. Bring to a boil; reduce heat to low and simmer.

Meanwhile, in a liquid measuring cup, beat egg. Add enough milk to measure 1 cup.

In a medium bowl, combine flour, baking powder, parsley and salt. Stir in egg-milk mixture just until flour is moistened. (Dough will be soft and sticky.)

Dip a large metal spoon into the simmering liquid, then scoop up spoonfuls of batter and drop into soup. Repeat until all the batter is dropped onto the soup. Return liquid to simmer, cover and simmer for 10 minutes.

Serve dumplings and sauce with every kind of meat — chicken, turkey, lamb, beef or pork. Makes 8 (3-inch) dumplings.

*Can also be made with cream of chicken or Cheddar cheese soup. If you wish more sauce (there is only enough to coat dumplings), double the amount of soup and water.

Mary Kay McElroy
Kremmling, CO

Mary Kay McElroy

YEAST PANCAKES

"I usually serve these with maple syrup, whipped butter and sausage. The batter keeps well for up to five days and is very good made in the waffle iron as well."

1½ cups buttermilk	3 tablespoons sugar
3 eggs	1 package active dry yeast
¼ cup vegetable oil	1 teaspoon baking powder
1 teaspoon vanilla extract	1 teaspoon baking soda
2 cups all-purpose flour	¼ teaspoon salt

continued on next page . . .

Yeast Pancakes continued . . .

In a medium bowl, mix buttermilk, eggs, oil and vanilla until well blended.

In a large mixer bowl, stir flour, sugar, yeast, baking powder, baking soda and salt. At low speed, gradually beat in buttermilk mixture until blended. At medium speed, beat for 2 minutes. Let stand at room temperature for 1 hour. Cover and refrigerate overnight.

To cook pancakes, stir down the mixture. Over medium heat, bake on a lightly greased hot griddle until bubbles appear and break; turn and brown lightly. For a thinner pancake, add a little milk just before baking. Makes 24 (3 inches each).

Kathy Foster
Appleton City, MO

BACON-ONION OATMEAL BUNS

(pictured on page 15)

"A different idea for these buns is to cut them in half and fill with mayonnaise, cooked chicken or ham, alfalfa sprouts, sunflower seeds and Swiss cheese."

2 cups boiling water
1 cup quick-cooking oats
1 package (12 oz.) bacon, cut in ¼-inch pieces
2 cups chopped onions
2 packages active dry yeast
⅓ cup warm water (105° to 115°)
⅔ cup packed brown sugar
¼ cup light or dark molasses
3 tablespoons vegetable oil
1 egg
2 teaspoons salt
6 to 7 cups all-purpose flour
Melted butter

In a large bowl, stir together boiling water and oats; let cool.

In a 10-inch skillet over medium heat, fry bacon until lightly browned. With a slotted spoon, transfer bacon pieces to paper towels; set aside. Pour off all but 3 tablespoons of the drippings. Sauté onions in drippings for 4 to 5 minutes or until golden brown. Transfer onions to paper towels; set aside.

Meanwhile, in a small bowl, dissolve yeast in warm water.

To the oats, add yeast mixture, brown sugar, molasses, oil, egg and salt, stirring until combined. Beat in 2½ cups of the flour. Stir in bacon and onions. Gradually add flour to form a soft dough. On a lightly floured surface, knead until smooth and elastic. Place in a greased bowl; turn to coat surface. Cover and let rise in a warm place, free from drafts, until doubled, about 1 to 1½ hours. Punch down dough; cover, let rise until doubled, 20 to 30 minutes.

Grease two 9×9×2-inch baking pans. Punch down dough. Make 32 balls, using about ⅓ cup of dough for each. Place in baking pans. Cover and let rise in a warm place, free from drafts, until doubled, about 20 to 30 minutes. Bake in a preheated 375° oven for 25 to 30 minutes or until golden brown. Brush with butter. Serve warm. Makes 32.

Jeanette K. Kurtz
Mandan, ND

HONEY-OATMEAL WHITE BREAD

(pictured on page 15)

"The bread is best served warm or toasted with butter and homemade jam or marmalade. I like the texture from the old-fashioned oats."

2 packages active dry yeast	2 teaspoons salt
½ cup warm water (105° to 115°)	2¼ cups old-fashioned oats
4 cups milk, scalded	⅓ cup wheat germ (optional)
5 tablespoons butter or margarine	9½ cups all-purpose flour
5 tablespoons honey	Melted butter
	Additional oats

Grease three 9×5×3-inch loaf pans or four 8½×4½×2½-inch loaf pans. In a small bowl, dissolve yeast in water.

In a large bowl, stir together milk, butter or margarine, honey and salt until butter or margarine is melted. Let cool to 115°. Stir in yeast mixture, oats and wheat germ. Stir in 9 cups of the flour until well mixed (dough will be sticky). On a floured surface, knead dough with additional ½ cup flour until smooth and elastic, 8 to 10 minutes.

Divide dough into three or four equal portions. Shape each into a loaf and place in pans. Cover and let rise in a warm place, free from drafts, until doubled, 1 to 1½ hours. Bake in the lower third of a preheated 350° oven for 45 to 55 minutes or until loaves sound hollow when bottoms are tapped. Cover with foil after first 30 minutes of baking to prevent excessive browning. Immediately remove from pans; brush with butter and sprinkle with oats. Cool on sides on wire racks. Makes 3 large or 4 medium loaves.

Elizabeth Barnes Schroeder
Hockessin, DE

Elizabeth Barnes Schroeder

APPLE-CARROT QUICK BREAD

1¾ cups all-purpose flour	½ cup shredded carrot
⅔ cup sugar	¼ cup butter or margarine, softened
1 teaspoon baking powder	
1 teaspoon baking soda	2 eggs
½ teaspoon salt	½ teaspoon lemon extract (optional)
1½ cups peeled, shredded tart apples (about 2 medium)	½ cup flaked coconut

Preheat oven to 350°. Grease bottom of an 8½×4½×2½-inch loaf pan. In a medium bowl, combine flour, sugar, baking powder, baking soda and salt; set aside.

continued on next page . . .

Apple-Carrot Quick Bread continued . . .

In a large mixer bowl at low speed, beat apples, carrot, butter or margarine, eggs and lemon extract until well blended. Add flour mixture and coconut; beat until well moistened. Spread in pan. Bake for 50 to 60 minutes or until a wooden pick inserted in center comes out clean. Remove from pan; cool on a wire rack. Makes 1 loaf.

Dawn M. Beneway
Poughquag, NY

SOUR CREAM ROLLS

"My mother passed this recipe down to me. The rolls are light and fluffy with a rich topping. They're best made with farm fresh cream if available."

1 package active dry yeast	1 teaspoon salt
¼ cup warm water (105° to 115°)	⅛ teaspoon baking soda
1 cup dairy sour cream	½ cup packed brown sugar
3 tablespoons sugar	3 teaspoons ground cinnamon
1 tablespoon butter or margarine, softened	¼ cup butter or margarine, melted
1 egg	1 cup sugar
3 cups all-purpose flour	¾ cup whipping cream

In a small bowl, dissolve yeast in water.

In a large mixer bowl at medium speed, beat sour cream, 3 tablespoons sugar and softened butter or margarine until blended. Add yeast mixture and egg; beat until well blended. Add flour, salt and baking soda. Beat at low speed until well blended.

On a lightly floured surface, knead until smooth and elastic, 5 to 8 minutes. Cover and let rest for 15 minutes.

Lightly grease two 8×8×2-inch baking pans. In a small bowl, mix brown sugar and 1 teaspoon of the cinnamon; set aside.

On a lightly floured surface, roll dough into an 18×8-inch rectangle. Brush with melted butter or margarine and sprinkle with the brown sugar mixture. Starting from long side, roll as for a jelly roll. Cut into 1-inch slices. Place nine slices, cut-side down, in each baking pan. Cover and let rise in a warm place, free from drafts, until doubled, 45 minutes to 1 hour.

Meanwhile, in a small saucepan, mix 1 cup sugar and remaining 2 teaspoons cinnamon. Stir in cream. Over medium heat, bring to a boil; reduce heat to low and simmer for 3 minutes. Cool slightly. Pour over rolls just before baking. Bake in a preheated 375° oven for 15 to 20 minutes or until golden brown. Cool in pans on wire racks for 5 minutes. Invert onto wire racks over waxed paper; remove pans. Makes 18.

Ruth G. Doxon
Des Moines, IA

MOLASSES CRUMB MUFFINS

"These moist, sweet muffins are great for breakfast, but also good as a dessert with coffee, tea or milk. They won first prize in the 1981 Warren County Farmer's Fair."

1 cup milk	1 teaspoon ground cinnamon
1 tablespoon cider vinegar	½ teaspoon salt
2 cups all-purpose flour	1 teaspoon baking soda
1 cup sugar	1 teaspoon ground ginger
½ cup solid vegetable shortening	2 tablespoons light molasses

Preheat oven to 350°. Line eighteen muffin-pan cups with paper liners. In a small bowl, mix milk and vinegar; set aside.

In a large bowl, mix flour, sugar, shortening, cinnamon and salt until crumbly. Reserve ¾ cup of the crumb mixture for topping.

To remaining flour mixture, add baking soda and ginger; stir to combine. Stir in milk mixture and molasses just until flour is moistened. Fill paper liners half full. Sprinkle with reserved crumb mixture. Bake for 20 to 25 minutes or until lightly browned around edges and a wooden pick inserted in center comes out clean. Serve warm. Makes 18.

Dawn M. Barretto
Stewartsville, NJ

SAVORY PICNIC SNAK BREAD

(pictured on page 15)

"This pull-apart bread is savory with herbs and cheese. It's a good companion to picnic fare and travels well."

1 cup dairy sour cream	2 tablespoons solid vegetable shortening
1 package active dry yeast	
¼ cup warm water (105° to 115°)	1 teaspoon salt
2¼ cups all-purpose flour	1½ cups grated Parmesan cheese
1 egg	2 tablespoons chopped parsley
2 tablespoons sugar	
2 tablespoons chopped chives	1½ teaspoons paprika
	½ cup butter, melted

In a small saucepan over low heat, warm sour cream to 105°.

In a large mixer bowl, dissolve yeast in water. Add sour cream, 1½ cups of the flour, egg, sugar, chives, shortening and salt. At low speed, beat until blended, then beat 1 minute longer. Stir in remaining ¾ cup flour until well mixed. Cover and let rise in a warm place, free from drafts, until doubled, about 45 minutes.

continued on next page . . .

Savory Picnic Snak Bread continued . . .

Generously grease a 10-inch tube pan. In a small bowl, mix cheese, parsley and paprika; set aside.

Stir down dough. Drop by rounded ½ tablespoons onto waxed paper, forming forty-eight 1-inch balls. Dip each ball in butter, then roll in cheese mixture. Place balls ¼ inch apart in layers in pan. Pour any remaining butter over top; sprinkle with any remaining cheese mixture. Cover and let rise in a warm place, free from drafts, until doubled, 20 to 30 minutes. Bake in a preheated 400° oven for 20 to 30 minutes or until golden brown. Cool in pan on a wire rack for 5 minutes; remove from pan. Serve warm. Makes 8 to 10 servings.

Jean Roetter
Melrose, WI

SOME KIND OF A CHEESECAKE

"My husband asked a typist to type a copy of the recipe to send to you. She asked him for the title. He said, 'I don't know. All I know is it's some kind of a cheesecake.' So that's the way she typed it!"

1 package active dry yeast	2 packages (8 oz. each) cream cheese, softened
1 tablespoon sugar	
¼ cup warm milk (105° to 115°)	1 cup sugar
2⅓ cups all-purpose flour	1 egg yolk
½ teaspoon salt	1 teaspoon vanilla extract
1 cup butter	1 egg white, lightly beaten
4 egg yolks, beaten	¼ cup chopped walnuts

In a small bowl, dissolve yeast and 1 tablespoon sugar in warm milk; let stand until foamy, 5 to 10 minutes.

In a large bowl, combine flour and salt. With a pastry blender or two knives, cut in butter until mixture resembles coarse crumbs.

Add 4 egg yolks to yeast mixture and stir until blended. Stir into flour mixture until well blended; set aside.

In a small mixer bowl at medium speed, beat cream cheese, 1 cup sugar, 1 egg yolk and vanilla until smooth and fluffy; set aside.

Divide dough in half. On a lightly floured surface, roll one portion into a 10-inch circle. Place on an ungreased baking sheet. Spoon filling in center and spread to within 1 inch of edge. Roll second portion of dough into a 10-inch circle. Place on top of filling, press edges to seal. Brush top with egg white. Sprinkle with nuts. Cover and let rise in a warm place, free from drafts, until doubled, about 2 hours.

Bake in a preheated 350° oven for 30 minutes or until golden brown. Cool completely on a wire rack. Serve or cover and chill until 1 hour before serving. Makes 16 to 20 servings.

Ruth Kush
Mundelein, IL

MAMA'S CHOCOLATE CINNAMON ROLLS

"I developed this recipe while I was a dietician at the Kansas State School for the Blind in the early 1960s. The children liked the unusual chocolate taste that distinguished these from all the other sweet rolls they usually received."

1 package active dry yeast	2 eggs
1 cup warm water (105° to 115°)	¼ cup butter or margarine, melted
4 cups all-purpose flour	½ cup sugar
½ cup unsweetened cocoa powder	1 tablespoon ground cinnamon
¼ cup nonfat dry milk powder	½ cup sugar
½ teaspoon salt	⅓ cup water
¾ cup sugar	Powdered Sugar Glaze (see below)
½ cup solid vegetable shortening or margarine	½ cup chopped nuts

In a small bowl, dissolve yeast in 1 cup warm water.

In a large bowl, combine flour, cocoa powder, dry milk and salt; set aside.

In a large mixer bowl at medium speed, beat ¾ cup sugar and shortening or margarine for 2 minutes or until fluffy. Add eggs and mix well. Stir in yeast mixture. Gradually stir flour mixture into yeast mixture to form a soft dough. Place in a greased bowl; turn to coat surface. Cover and let rise in a warm place, free from drafts, until doubled, about 45 minutes.

Grease two baking sheets. Punch down dough. On a lightly floured surface, roll into an 18 × 12-inch rectangle. Brush with melted butter or margarine. In a small bowl, mix ½ cup sugar and cinnamon. Sprinkle sugar mixture over the dough. Starting from the long side, roll as for a jelly roll. Cut into twenty-four ¾-inch slices; place cut-side down on baking sheets. Cover and let rise until almost doubled, about 30 minutes. Bake in a preheated 350° oven for 18 to 22 minutes or until bottoms of rolls sound hollow when tapped.

Meanwhile, in a small saucepan over medium heat, cook and stir ½ cup sugar and ⅓ cup water until sugar is completely dissolved. Generously brush over hot rolls. Cool. Glaze top of rolls with Powdered Sugar Glaze and sprinkle with nuts. Best eaten the same day. Makes 24.

POWDERED SUGAR GLAZE

2 cups powdered sugar	Pinch of salt
1 tablespoon solid vegetable shortening	¼ cup water
	½ teaspoon vanilla extract

In a small mixer bowl at low speed, beat powdered sugar, shortening and salt until blended. Add water and vanilla; beat until smooth. Makes 1¼ cups.

Lottie H. Polk
Kansas City, KS

Salads and Side Dishes

SURPRISE SALAD

"I love to cook and entertain. This is a pretty luncheon main dish salad at Christmas time because of the red and green color combination."

3 cups boiling water	Lettuce leaves
2 packages (3 oz. each) cherry gelatin	Chicken Salad (see below)
	Paprika
1 cup dairy sour cream	Parsley sprigs
1 can (16 oz.) whole berry cranberry sauce	

In a medium bowl, pour water over gelatin; stir until dissolved. Stir in sour cream until smooth. Stir in cranberry sauce until blended. Pour into a 6-cup ring mold. Chill at least 4 hours or overnight.

Unmold salad onto lettuce-lined serving platter. Fill center with chicken salad and sprinkle chicken with paprika. If some chicken salad remains, place small mounds around base of mold. Garnish platter with parsley. Makes 8 to 10 servings.

CHICKEN SALAD

1 cup mayonnaise	5 cups cubed cooked chicken
3 tablespoons lemon juice	1 cup chopped celery
1½ teaspoons salt	½ cup toasted chopped pecans
½ teaspoon pepper	

In a large bowl, mix mayonnaise, lemon juice, salt and pepper. Stir in chicken and celery. Cover and chill or serve immediately, stirring in nuts just before serving. Makes 5 cups.

Jean Turner
Plano, TX

Pictured on the preceding page, top to bottom, are Easy Refrigerator Pickles (see page 35), Sweet and Sour Carrots (see page 28), and Chicken Salad Helene (see page 36).

AVOCADO SALAD

"This salad is a colorful beginning to a meal and it goes well with practically any type of food."

8 slices bacon	2 to 3 medium avocados,
½ cup finely chopped onion	peeled and cubed (about
¼ cup cider vinegar	2 cups)
1 teaspoon lemon juice	Lettuce leaves
¾ teaspoon salt	Tomato wedges
¼ teaspoon pepper	

In a 10-inch skillet over medium heat, fry bacon until crisp. With a slotted spoon, transfer bacon to paper towels; crumble and set aside. Pour off all but 2 tablespoons of the drippings. Over low heat, sauté onion in drippings for 3 minutes. Add vinegar, lemon juice, salt and pepper. Simmer for 3 minutes or until onion is tender. Add bacon and remove from heat.

Pour dressing over avocados. Toss lightly. Serve on lettuce and garnish with tomato if desired. Makes 4 servings.

Sheri Kinler
Joplin, MO

BAKED MUSHROOMS

"I usually serve this dish with steak, but it is also good with just a salad and bread."

1 pound mushrooms, sliced	Dash of ground white
2 tablespoons minced onion	pepper
3 tablespoons butter or	2 teaspoons chopped fresh
margarine	dill or ¾ teaspoon dried
¼ cup grated Parmesan	dill weed
cheese	1 cup whipping cream
1 tablespoon all-purpose	2 egg yolks, lightly beaten
flour	3 tablespoons fine soft bread
¼ teaspoon salt	crumbs

Preheat oven to 425°. Butter a shallow 1-quart baking dish. In a large skillet over medium-low heat, stir mushrooms and onion in butter or margarine until vegetables are coated. Cover and simmer for 8 minutes. Add cheese, flour, salt and pepper; cook and stir for 2 to 3 minutes. Pour into baking dish. Sprinkle with dill.

In a small bowl, mix cream and egg yolks until well blended. Pour over mushrooms. Sprinkle with bread crumbs. Bake for 12 to 15 minutes or until set. Serve immediately. Makes 6 (½-cup) servings.

Judy McCann
Collinsville, IL

SWEET AND SOUR CARROTS

(pictured on page 25)

"My daughter and I classify our recipe as a salad and a good dish to take along on picnics."

1 pound carrots, peeled and diagonally sliced ¼ inch thick	⅓ cup sugar
	1 tablespoon cornstarch
	½ teaspoon salt
1 medium green pepper, cut in ¾-inch pieces	2 tablespoons cider vinegar
	2 teaspoons soy sauce
1 can (8 oz.) pineapple tidbits or chunks	Watercress (optional)

In a covered 2-quart saucepan, cook carrots in boiling salted water for 15 to 20 minutes or until tender. Add green pepper and cook 3 minutes longer. Drain and set aside.

Drain pineapple juice into a measuring cup; add water to measure ⅓ cup liquid. Reserve pineapple.

In a small saucepan, combine sugar, cornstarch and salt. Stir in pineapple liquid, vinegar and soy sauce until smooth. Stirring over medium heat, bring to a boil and boil for 1 to 2 minutes or until thickened. Pour over carrots and green pepper. Stir in pineapple. Heat through to serve hot as a side dish or cool and serve at room temperature as a salad. Garnish with watercress if desired. Makes 6 to 8 servings.

Mrs. Jessie N. Smith
Parkersburg, WV

TURNIPS TERRIFIC

"When my neighbors kept sharing their big crop of turnips with us, I decided that it was time to invent a way to cook turnips so they tasted good. You can only eat so many raw! This turned out so well I couldn't call it just Turnip Casserole."

2 pounds turnips, peeled and cubed	1½ cups milk
¾ teaspoon salt	6 ounces pasteurized process cheese spread, cubed
2 teaspoons sugar	4 slices bacon
⅛ teaspoon pepper	2 slices whole wheat bread, cubed
⅛ teaspoon paprika	1 cup coarsely crushed sour cream and onion potato chips
2 tablespoons butter or margarine	
3 tablespoons all-purpose flour	

continued on next page . . .

Turnips Terrific continued . . .

Preheat oven to 350°. Grease a shallow 2-quart baking dish. In a large saucepan, place turnips and ½ teaspoon of the salt in 1 inch of water. Over high heat, bring to a boil; reduce heat to low, cover and simmer for 10 minutes or until tender. Drain well and set aside.

In a small bowl, mix remaining ¼ teaspoon salt, sugar, pepper and paprika; set aside.

In a 1-quart saucepan over medium heat, melt butter or margarine. Stir in flour. Cook and stir for 1 to 2 minutes. Stir in sugar mixture. Stir in milk. Stirring, bring to a boil and boil until thickened. Stir in cheese until melted; set aside.

In a large skillet over medium heat, fry bacon until crisp. With a slotted spoon, transfer bacon to paper towels, crumble and set aside. Pour off all but 1 tablespoon of the drippings. Over medium-high heat, sauté bread cubes in drippings for 2 to 3 minutes or until lightly toasted.

To the turnips, add cheese sauce, bacon and bread cubes and stir gently. Pour into baking dish. Top with chips. Bake for 20 to 30 minutes or until lightly browned and bubbly. Makes 6 to 8 servings.

Janet Randolph
Topeka, KS

PLOWMAN'S SHARE

"You can also use this hearty side dish as a vegetarian entrée."

1 package (10 oz.) frozen chopped broccoli
1 package (10 oz.) frozen cauliflower
¼ cup diced onion
½ cup butter or margarine
¼ pound mushrooms, sliced
½ cup chopped green pepper
3 tablespoons soy sauce
3 large russet potatoes, baked and kept hot
1 cup shredded sharp Cheddar cheese

Preheat oven to 300°. In a large saucepan, cook broccoli and cauliflower according to package directions; drain. Cut cauliflower into bite-size pieces. Set vegetables aside.

Meanwhile, in a large skillet over medium heat, sauté onion in butter or margarine for 3 minutes. Add mushrooms, green pepper and soy sauce. Sauté until vegetables are tender.

Cut potatoes in half lengthwise. Place in a shallow 2½-quart baking dish or individual ramekins. Spoon broccoli-cauliflower mixture evenly on top of potatoes, packing lightly. Top with mushroom mixture and sprinkle with cheese. Bake for 5 to 7 minutes or until cheese melts. Makes 6 servings.

Rebecca L. Herrera
Aurora, CO

LEMON-CREAM CHEESE SALAD

"This firm salad holds well so it's especially good for picnics and potlucks."

2 cups boiling water
1 package (6 oz.) lemon
  gelatin
3 tablespoons sugar (optional)
1 package (8 oz.) cream
  cheese, softened
1 can (20 oz.) crushed
  pineapple in its own
  juice, undrained

2 cups chopped apples
  (Winesap, Red or Golden
  Delicious)
2 ribs celery, diced
½ cup coarsely chopped
  walnuts
Lettuce leaves

In a medium bowl, pour water over gelatin and sugar; stir until dissolved. In a large mixer bowl at medium speed, beat cream cheese until fluffy. At low speed, slowly add gelatin mixture and beat until smooth. Stir in pineapple, apples, celery and nuts. Pour into a 13×9×2-inch baking pan. Cover and chill at least 4 hours or overnight.

Cut and serve on lettuce if desired. Makes 12 servings.

Mrs. Maurice Tate
Beaver Falls, PA

SWEET POTATO-STUFFED PEACH HALVES

"This is the only way my family will eat sweet potatoes. I've also used orange liqueur in place of the sherry. Make extra if serving to company as they usually want seconds! It is especially good with chicken, turkey or ham."

1 cup mashed cooked sweet
  potatoes
2 tablespoons brown sugar
1½ tablespoons sherry
  (optional)
1½ tablespoons frozen orange
  juice concentrate
¼ teaspoon salt

⅛ teaspoon ground cloves
6 canned peach halves, well
  drained
2 tablespoons butter or
  margarine
12 pecan halves
6 maraschino cherries

Preheat oven to 400°. Butter an 8×8×2-inch baking dish. In a small mixer bowl at low speed, beat sweet potatoes, brown sugar, sherry, orange juice concentrate, salt and cloves until well blended. Mound about ¼ cup of the mixture in center of each peach half. Place in baking dish. Top each with 1 teaspoon of the butter or margarine. Bake for 20 minutes or until heated through.

Place 2 pecan halves and a cherry on top of each potato mound. Makes 6 servings.

Olive C. Jeblick
Albuquerque, NM

DATE SALAD

"As a holiday salad, place a slice of jellied cranberry sauce on a lettuce leaf and top with a spoonful of Date Salad. This recipe was handed down from my grandmother to my mother to me."

1 cup whipping cream
2 packages (3 oz. each)
   cream cheese, softened
¼ teaspoon vanilla extract
1 package (8 oz.) chopped
   dates

1 can (8 oz.) crushed pine-
   apple, well drained
1 cup chopped pecans
   Sugar (optional)
   Lettuce leaves
   Maraschino cherries

In a small mixer bowl at medium speed, beat whipping cream until stiff; set aside. In a small mixer bowl at low speed, beat cream cheese and vanilla until fluffy. Beat in whipped cream just until combined. By hand, stir in dates, pineapple and pecans. Sweeten to taste if desired. Cover and refrigerate at least 1 hour. Mound ⅓ cup mixture on a lettuce leaf and top with a cherry. Best served same day. Makes 12 servings.

Fairfax Montgomery
Athens, GA

CABBAGE SALAD

"There aren't many salads you can serve with Chinese food, but this is really good with it. It's both chewy and crunchy."

5 tablespoons cider vinegar
3 tablespoons sugar
1½ teaspoons salt
¾ teaspoon pepper
⅓ to ½ cup vegetable oil
1 whole chicken breast,
   cooked, skinned, boned
   and cut in thin strips
3½ cups finely shredded
   cabbage

2 tablespoons thinly sliced
   green onion, including tops
1 package (3 oz.) uncooked
   instant Chinese noodles
   (do not use seasoning
   packet), crumbled
3 tablespoons toasted sliced
   almonds
2 tablespoons toasted
   sesame seeds

In a small bowl, combine vinegar, sugar, salt, pepper and oil; cover and set aside.

Place chicken in a large salad bowl. Add cabbage and green onion; toss. Can be chilled up to 2 hours before serving if desired.

To serve, add noodles, almonds and sesame seeds to cabbage mixture. Stir dressing, pour over and toss. Makes 6 to 8 servings.

Kathleen Franzini
Pahrump, NV

31

CHINESE CUCUMBER SALAD

"I serve this light, refreshing salad with more hearty dishes. It can be made ahead and frees me to work on other parts of the meal. It's a good accompaniment to a barbecue."

1 tablespoon sugar	1 medium clove garlic, crushed
1 tablespoon rice vinegar or white wine vinegar	2 medium cucumbers
2 teaspoons vegetable oil	¼ cup sliced green onions
2 teaspoons soy sauce	¼ cup toasted sesame seeds*
1¼ teaspoons chili powder	Tomato rose (optional)
	Parsley sprig (optional)

In a 1½-quart bowl, combine sugar, vinegar, oil, soy sauce, chili powder and garlic until well blended.

Peel cucumbers if skin is tough and cut cucumbers in half lengthwise. With a melon baller or small spoon, scoop out seeds. Cut into ¼-inch thick slices. (You should have about 2¼ cups.) Add to dressing and stir until well coated. Cover and chill at least 2 hours.

Just before serving, remove garlic and stir in green onions and sesame seeds. Garnish with tomato rose and parsley. Makes 4 (about ½-cup) servings.

*To toast seeds, place in a pie plate. Bake in a preheated 350° oven for 8 to 10 minutes or until golden brown; cool.

Mary Lou Denison
Los Angeles, CA

Mary Lou Denison

STUFFED ONIONS

"Stuffed Onions are good as a side dish with poultry or pork, but I also serve them as a luncheon dish along with salad and rolls."

4 large onions	1 teaspoon chopped chives or parsley (optional)
1½ teaspoons salt	¼ teaspoon pepper
1 cup soft bread crumbs	¼ teaspoon celery seeds (optional)
1 can (4 oz.) mushroom pieces and stems, drained and chopped	3 tablespoons butter or margarine, melted
4 slices bacon, fried crisp and crumbled, 2 tablespoons drippings reserved	Chopped chives or parsley sprigs

continued on next page . . .

Stuffed Onions continued . . .

Peel onions, leaving root end intact. Cut in half lengthwise. Place in a 3-quart saucepan. Add water to a depth of 1 inch. Add 1 teaspoon of the salt and over medium heat, bring to a boil; reduce heat to low, cover and simmer for 15 to 20 minutes or until almost tender. Drain and cool slightly.

Preheat oven to 350°. Remove centers of onions, leaving a ½-inch shell; chop centers. In a medium bowl, gently stir chopped onions, bread crumbs, mushrooms, bacon, 1 teaspoon chives or parsley, remaining ½ teaspoon salt, pepper and celery seeds.

Pour butter or margarine into an 8×8×2-inch baking pan. Place onion shells, rounded-side down, in pan. Brush with butter or margarine. Mound stuffing mixture into center of onions, packing lightly. Drizzle tops with bacon drippings. Bake for 20 to 30 minutes or until tops are lightly browned. Garnish with chives or parsley. Makes 8 servings.

Jo Ann Townsend
Waterloo, IA

SPINACH-RICE SALAD

"Here's a perfect do-ahead recipe which is good for buffets. It's an easy and inexpensive dish that I have never had anyone dislike."

1⅓ cups water	⅓ cup frozen peas, thawed
⅔ cup long grain rice	¼ cup finely chopped green
½ bay leaf	onions, including some
1 teaspoon lemon juice	tops
½ teaspoon salt	1 jar (2 oz.) sliced pimiento,
½ cup Italian salad dressing	drained
2 cups torn fresh spinach	2 tablespoons chopped
leaves	parsley
1 medium tomato, seeded	⅛ teaspoon pepper
and cubed	4 slices bacon, fried crisp and
⅓ cup diced green pepper	crumbled

In a 1-quart saucepan over high heat, bring water to a boil, reduce heat to low. Stir in rice, bay leaf, lemon juice and salt; cover and simmer for 20 to 25 minutes or until rice is tender and moisture is absorbed. Remove bay leaf. Toss rice with ¼ cup of the salad dressing; cover and refrigerate until cool.

Meanwhile, in a separate large bowl, combine spinach, tomato, green pepper, peas, green onions, pimiento, parsley and pepper. Toss with remaining ¼ cup salad dressing. Add rice and toss gently. Cover and chill for 2 hours.

Just before serving, sprinkle with bacon. Makes 4 to 6 servings.

Linda Bliss
Mission Viejo, CA

RICE-CHEESE BAKE

"This is a delicate rice casserole with a bit of spicy flavor. It makes a lot — which is good for family get-togethers and potlucks."

1 cup long grain rice	½ teaspoon salt
3 medium zucchini, sliced	2 cups dairy sour cream
1 can (7 oz.) whole green chilies, drained and coarsley chopped	¼ cup chopped green pepper
	¼ cup chopped green onions
12 ounces Monterey Jack cheese, shredded	1 teaspoon dried oregano leaves, crushed
1 large tomato, peeled (if desired) and thinly sliced	1 teaspoon garlic salt
	2 tablespoons chopped parsley

Cook rice according to package directions. Preheat oven to 350°. Butter a 3-quart baking dish.

Meanwhile, in a second saucepan, cook zucchini in a small amount of boiling salted water until crisp-tender. Drain and set aside.

In baking dish, layer rice, green chilies, 1½ cups of the cheese and the tomato slices. Sprinkle with ½ teaspoon salt. Top with zucchini.

In a small bowl, stir sour cream, green pepper, green onions, oregano and garlic salt. Spoon over tomato slices. Sprinkle with remaining cheese. Bake for 35 to 45 minutes or until bubbly around the edges. Garnish with parsley before serving. Makes 10 to 12 servings.

Kathryn J. Umland
Nebraska City, NE

GRANDMA'S YELLOW SQUASH SURPRISE

"I decided to fix squash so everyone would like it after hearing 'Ugh, squash!' again. My recipe is based on the cheesy grits recipe which is so popular here. The 'surprise' is that the grandchildren liked it — and so have all of my friends who have tried it."

2 pounds yellow summer squash or zucchini, cut in pieces	¼ cup margarine
	2 eggs
½ cup water	½ cup evaporated milk
6 ounces garlic pasteurized process cheese spread, cut in ½-inch pieces	1 tablespoon all-purpose flour
	1 teaspoon sugar
	½ cup coarse cracker crumbs

continued on next page . . .

Grandma's Yellow Squash Surprise continued . . .

Preheat oven to 325°. Grease an 8×8×2-inch baking dish. In a large saucepan over medium-high heat, bring squash and water to a boil; reduce heat to low and simmer for 15 minutes or until squash is tender. Drain off all but ½ cup of the liquid. Mash squash slightly. Add cheese and margarine; stir until cheese is melted. Remove from heat.

Add eggs, evaporated milk, flour and sugar; stir until blended. Pour into baking dish. Top with crumbs. Bake for 30 minutes or until set. Makes 8 (¾-cup) servings.

Mary-Margaret Bates Brown
Roanoke, VA

EASY REFRIGERATOR PICKLES

(pictured on page 25)

"Just like the old-fashioned bread and butter pickles without the fuss! An excellent homemade condiment for lunches, picnics, or as part of a relish tray for dinner. Great Christmas gift!"

6 cups thinly sliced unpeeled small cucumbers*	½ teaspoon salt
	½ teaspoon celery seeds
2 cups thinly sliced onions	½ teaspoon mustard seeds
1½ cups sugar	½ teaspoon ground turmeric
1½ cups white vinegar	

In a 2½-quart glass bowl or gallon jar, alternately layer cucumbers and onions.

In a 2-quart non-aluminum saucepan, combine sugar, vinegar, salt, celery seeds, mustard seeds and turmeric. Stirring over medium heat, bring to a boil and boil until sugar is dissolved. Pour over cucumbers and onions; stir. Cool for 10 minutes. Cover tightly and refrigerate for 24 hours, stirring occasionally. Makes about 2 quarts.

*Two cups cauliflowerets can be substituted for 2 cups of the cucumbers. One 4-ounce jar sliced pimientos, drained, can be added if desired.

Marylee Evans
Carolina, RI

CHICKEN SALAD HELENE

(pictured on page 25)

"I love to cook and create new recipes — especially soups and salads. Current's cookbooks are frequently my inspiration as Director of Food Service for my church. This recipe is one I invented for the church's 'Family Table' where salads are popular with the staff and volunteer workers."

6 cups coarsely shredded iceberg lettuce
6 cups torn fresh spinach leaves
Special Dressing (see below)
1 package (6 oz.) frozen snow peas
3 boneless chicken breast halves, cooked and chilled

1 can (8 oz.) sliced water chestnuts, well drained
½ pound mushrooms, sliced
1 small avocado, peeled and cut in ½-inch slices
¼ cup thinly sliced green onions
2 ounces alfalfa sprouts (about 1½ cups)
8 ounces bacon, fried crisp and crumbled

In a large bowl, toss together lettuce and spinach; chill.

Prepare Special Dressing and chill at least 15 minutes or until ready to use.

Cook snow peas in boiling salted water for 1 minute or until crisp-tender. Immediately plunge into cold water until chilled; drain well.

Cut chicken into bite-size strips.

On a large platter or six large salad plates, arrange greens, snow peas, water chestnuts, mushrooms, avocado, green onions and sprouts. Top with chicken and bacon. Serve dressing separately. Makes 6 (2-cup) servings.

SPECIAL DRESSING

½ cup cider vinegar
½ cup vegetable oil
2 tablespoons brown sugar
2 tablespoons sliced green onion

2 teaspoons Dijon mustard
1 teaspoon seasoned salt
¼ teaspoon pepper

In a blender container, place vinegar, oil, brown sugar, green onion, mustard, seasoned salt and pepper; cover. Blend at high speed for 2 minutes or until smooth and creamy.

Cover and refrigerate until ready to serve. Makes about 1¼ cups.

Helen L. Mahon
Darien, CT

Meat Main Dishes

PIÑÓN

"Piñón is a favorite dish in Puerto Rico and is usually used for special holidays — much like turkey in the U.S. But it can be made at any time of year. The ripe plantains give the main taste to the dish."

2 slices bacon, cut in 1-inch pieces
3 large ripe plantains or 4 firm bananas, peeled and sliced lengthwise
2 to 3 tablespoons vegetable oil or bacon fat
½ pound lean ground beef
½ cup chopped onion
1 small clove garlic, minced
1 teaspoon dried oregano leaves, crushed
½ teaspoon salt
⅛ teaspoon pepper
1 can (8 oz.) tomato sauce
1 can (8 oz.) cut green beans, drained
2 hard-cooked eggs, chopped
1 tablespoon raisins
1 can (4 oz.) diced green chilies (optional)
¼ cup chopped ham (optional)
Sliced stuffed olives (optional)
4 eggs, beaten

Preheat oven to 350°. Lightly grease bottom of a 9×5×3-inch loaf pan. In a 10-inch skillet over medium heat, fry bacon until crisp; remove bacon and set aside. Sauté plantains or bananas in oil or bacon fat for 2 minutes on each side or until lightly browned. Remove and set aside.

In same skillet over medium heat, sauté ground beef, onion, garlic, oregano, salt and pepper until meat loses its pink color. Drain off fat. Stir in tomato sauce, green beans, hard-cooked eggs, bacon, raisins and any of the optional ingredients desired.

Layer in order: ½ of the beaten eggs, ⅓ of the plantains or bananas, ½ of the meat mixture, ⅓ of the plantains or bananas, remaining meat mixture, remaining plantains or bananas, and remaining beaten eggs. Bake for 30 to 40 minutes or until eggs are set and top is golden brown. Makes 4 to 6 servings.

Carol A. Dátil
Arecibo, PR

Pictured on the preceding page, top to bottom, are Spiced Pockets (see page 46), Baha's Mexican Batter Meatballs (see page 48), and Chinese Beef with Cheese (see page 46).

LAMB SHANKS

6 lamb shanks (3 to 4 lb.)
1 tablespoon solid vegetable
   shortening
1 can (10¾ oz.) condensed
   cream of mushroom soup
1 can (10½ oz.) condensed
   beef consommé

2 medium cloves garlic,
   minced
1 teaspoon browning and
   seasoning sauce
½ teaspoon Worcestershire
   sauce
¼ teaspoon maple flavor
   Hot cooked noodles

Preheat oven to 350°. In a 5-quart Dutch oven over medium-low heat, brown lamb shanks in shortening. Add soup, consommé, garlic, browning and seasoning sauce, Worcestershire sauce and maple flavor; stir to mix. Cover and bake for 1½ hours or until meat is tender. Skim fat from sauce; serve shanks and sauce over noodles. Makes 6 servings.

Joy T. Ayers
Roundup, MT

Joy T. Ayers

MICHAEL'S VENISON STEW

"My husband created this recipe. I never cared for venison until he developed this dish which hides the wild taste of the meat."

½ cup all-purpose flour
1 teaspoon salt
½ teaspoon pepper
½ teaspoon dried basil leaves,
   crushed
2 pounds lean venison or
   beef stew meat, cut in
   1-inch pieces
3 tablespoons solid vegetable
   shortening
1 quart tomato juice
5 medium onions, thinly
   sliced

1 cup dry red wine
6 to 8 medium carrots, cut in
   1-inch pieces
6 medium red potatoes,
   thinly sliced
1 cup thickly sliced celery
2 tablespoons quick-cooking
   tapioca
1 teaspoon Worcestershire
   sauce
2 to 3 small bay leaves

In a medium bowl, mix flour, salt, pepper and basil. Toss meat in flour mixture until evenly coated. In a 5-quart Dutch oven over medium heat, brown meat in shortening. Add tomato juice, onions and wine; bring to a boil. Transfer to a slow cooker. Add carrots, potatoes, celery, tapioca, Worcestershire sauce and bay leaves; stir to mix. Cover and cook on high for 5 hours or until meat and vegetables are tender. Makes 6 to 8 hearty servings.

Ann Bushman
Valders, WI

Ann Bushman

PICNIC CASSEROLE

"This is a good recipe to have ready in the summer months when my family members come home from playing softball. Nice with fruit salad."

4 medium red potatoes, peeled, diced and cooked
¼ cup butter or margarine, softened
2 tablespoons minced onion
6 frankfurters, sliced
1 can (10¾ oz.) condensed cream of mushroom soup
1 cup frozen peas, thawed
½ cup milk
1 tablespoon prepared mustard
⅓ cup shredded sharp Cheddar cheese

Preheat oven to 350°. In an ungreased 2-quart casserole, toss potatoes, butter or margarine, and onion. In a medium bowl, mix frankfurters, soup, peas, milk and mustard. Pour over potato mixture. Bake for 40 minutes. Top with cheese. Bake 5 minutes longer or until cheese melts. Makes 6 to 8 servings.

Jeanette F. Urbom
Dodge City, KS

CRUSTY LASAGNA

"I serve this unique lasagna on a platter garnished with parsley and cherry tomatoes. It has a tender, flaky crust and a very rich, meaty filling."

1 pound lean ground beef
¾ cup chopped onion
1 large clove garlic, minced
1 can (6 oz.) tomato paste
1 tablespoon dried parsley flakes
1 teaspoon dried basil leaves, crushed
¾ teaspoon salt
½ teaspoon dried oregano leaves, crushed
¼ teaspoon pepper
¾ cup margarine
1½ cups all-purpose flour
5 to 7 tablespoons cold water
1 egg
1 cup cottage cheese
⅓ cup grated Parmesan cheese
Milk
1 tablespoon sesame seeds

Preheat oven to 400°. In a 10-inch skillet over medium-high heat, brown beef, onion and garlic until onion is soft. Drain off fat. Stir in tomato paste, parsley, basil, salt, oregano and pepper. Simmer for 5 minutes.

continued on next page . . .

Crusty Lasagna continued . . .

Meanwhile, in a large bowl, cut margarine into flour with a pastry blender or two knives until pieces are the size of large peas. Sprinkle water over the top and mix with a fork until uniformly moistened and forms a ball. On a lightly floured surface, knead twelve times. Roll into a 15 × 13-inch rectangle. Transfer to an ungreased baking sheet.

In a small bowl, beat egg. Stir in cottage cheese and Parmesan cheese.

Spoon half of the meat mixture down center one-third of pastry to within 1 inch of short ends. Top with cottage cheese mixture and cover with remaining meat. Fold short ends of dough over filling, then fold long ends over, overlapping slightly. Press and pinch to seal edges. Brush surface with milk, being careful not to let milk drip onto baking sheet. Sprinkle with sesame seeds. Bake for 30 to 45 minutes or until golden brown. Makes 6 servings.

Norma J. Thigpin
Eagle Point, OR

DOG-GONES

"We heat Dog-Gones just before leaving for a football game, rodeo or baseball game, then pack them in our picnic basket. They stay hot for a long time."

1 **pound frankfurters, cut in ½-inch slices**	3 **tablespoons chopped green onions**
¾ **pound sharp Cheddar cheese, cubed**	3 **tablespoons mayonnaise**
3 **hard-cooked eggs, coarsely chopped**	1 **tablespoon catsup**
	8 **to 10 frankfurter buns**

Preheat oven to 400°. In a large bowl, mix frankfurters, cheese, eggs, green onions, mayonnaise and catsup. Evenly divide among frankfurter buns. Wrap each bun in foil. Bake for 15 minutes or until cheese is melted. Makes 8 to 10 servings.

Sandra Rohrich
Yakima, WA

MOCK BEEF BURGUNDY

"I was trying to come up with a meal I could serve company on a day I had to work. I created the sauce from several old recipes and went from there. I adjusted it several times until I was satisfied. I still vary the vegetables, but never the gravy itself."

2 pounds lean beef stew meat, cut in 1-inch pieces	½ pound mushrooms, cut in half
⅓ cup all-purpose flour	½ cup boiling water
1½ teaspoons salt	2 teaspoons beef bouillon granules
½ teaspoon dried thyme leaves, crushed	1 vegetable bouillon cube
¼ teaspoon pepper	1 cup cranberry juice
¼ teaspoon garlic powder	½ large bay leaf
3 carrots, cut in ½-inch slices	Hot cooked rice
1 cup chopped onion	

Place meat in a slow cooker. Sprinkle with flour, salt, thyme, pepper and garlic powder. Toss to coat meat. Add carrots, onion and mushrooms.

In a small bowl, stir water, beef bouillon granules and vegetable bouillon until bouillon is dissolved. Pour over vegetables. Add cranberry juice. Tuck bay leaf into center. Do not stir. Cover and cook at low heat for 8 to 10 hours or at high heat for 4 to 5 hours or until meat and vegetables are tender. Remove bay leaf before serving with rice. Makes 4 to 5 servings.

Barbara Anderson
Bisbee, AZ

Barbara Anderson

VEAL SUPREME

"You can use this mixture in crepes. Just cut the veal into smaller pieces."

2 pounds veal stew meat	½ cup dry sherry
4 to 5 tablespoons butter or margarine	1½ teaspoons Worcestershire sauce
1 can (10¾ oz.) condensed cream of mushroom soup	¼ to ½ teaspoon pepper
1 large onion, thinly sliced	½ to 1 cup dairy sour cream
½ pound mushrooms, sliced	Salt
½ cup water	Hot cooked noodles or rice

continued on next page . . .

Veal Supreme continued . . .

Preheat oven to 350°. In a 10-inch skillet over medium-high heat, brown a third of the meat at a time in 2 tablespoons of the butter or margarine, adding more butter or margarine as needed. Transfer meat to a Dutch oven or a 2½-quart baking dish. Spoon soup over meat; set aside.

In the same skillet, sauté onion in remaining butter or margarine until limp. Add mushrooms and sauté for 2 minutes. Transfer onions and mushrooms to baking dish.

Add water, sherry, Worcestershire sauce and pepper to skillet. Over medium-high heat, cook and scrape to loosen any browned bits from bottom of skillet. Pour over meat. Stir to blend sauce. Cover and bake for 45 minutes. Stir. Bake, uncovered, 30 minutes longer. Stir in sour cream and bake 10 minutes longer or until heated through (do not boil). Add salt if desired. Serve over noodles or rice. Makes 5 to 6 servings.

Jo Ann Uslick
Canton, OH

BIRD'S BEEF-NOODLE CASSEROLE

⅔ cup chopped onion	1 can (5.33 oz.) evaporated milk
½ cup chopped green pepper	1 tablespoon lemon juice
4 tablespoons butter or margarine, softened	1½ teaspoons Worcestershire sauce
1½ pounds lean ground beef	¼ teaspoon garlic powder
1 can (8 oz.) tomato sauce	¼ teaspoon salt
⅔ cup catsup	1 can (10¾ oz.) condensed cream of mushroom soup
½ pound mushrooms, sliced (optional)	1 package (12 oz.) medium egg noodles, broken, cooked and drained
1 package (8 oz.) cream cheese, softened	

Preheat oven to 375°. Grease a shallow 3-quart baking dish. In a 10-inch skillet over medium-high heat, sauté onion and green pepper in 2 tablespoons of the butter or margarine for 5 minutes or until tender. Add meat and brown. Drain off fat. Stir in tomato sauce, catsup and mushrooms. Cook for 5 to 10 minutes or until slightly thickened.

Meanwhile, in a large mixer bowl at low speed, beat cream cheese and remaining 2 tablespoons butter or margarine until fluffy. Beat in evaporated milk, lemon juice, Worcestershire sauce, garlic powder and salt. Stir in soup. Add noodles and stir until noodles are coated. Pour into baking dish. Top with meat mixture. Bake for 15 to 20 minutes or until bubbly and heated through. Makes 8 to 10 servings.

Mrs. Edna L. Bird
San Antonio, TX

STUFFED FLANK STEAK TERIYAKI

"This dish has been a hit even with those who say they don't like Oriental food."

1 to 1¼ pounds beef flank
   steak, ¾ inch thick
½ cup soy sauce
¼ cup vegetable oil
2 tablespoons brown sugar
2 teaspoons dry mustard
1 teaspoon ground ginger
⅛ teaspoon garlic powder

1 cup water
1 cup sliced mushrooms
1 can (8 oz.) sliced water
   chestnuts, drained
½ cup long grain rice
½ cup shredded carrot
¼ cup sliced green onions
Parsley sprigs

Cut a pocket lengthwise in flank steak. Place in a shallow baking dish.

In a small bowl, mix soy sauce, vegetable oil, brown sugar, mustard, ginger and garlic powder until well blended. Pour over meat, spooning some into pocket. Marinate for 30 minutes at room temperature, basting several times.

Meanwhile, in a medium saucepan over medium-high heat, bring water, mushrooms, water chestnuts, rice, carrot and green onions to a boil. Reduce heat to low, cover and simmer for 10 minutes or until rice is partially tender.

Preheat oven to 350°. Drain meat, reserving marinade. Fill steak with rice mixture. Secure with wooden picks. Place in a 12×8×2-inch glass baking dish. Cover with foil. Basting occasionally, bake for 1 to 1½ hours or until fork tender and edges are browned.

Transfer to a serving platter, slice across the grain and garnish with parsley. Makes 4 to 5 servings.

Elaine M. G. Ruth
Glen Burnie, MD

Elaine M. G. Ruth

PORK COVINGTON

8 loin pork chops, ¾ inch
   thick
Salt
Pepper
2 tablespoons butter or
   margarine
⅔ cup orange juice
½ cup raspberry preserves

½ cup dry sherry
½ teaspoon grated lemon
   rind
1 tablespoon lemon juice
2 teaspoons Dijon mustard
1 teaspoon ground ginger
½ teaspoon dry mustard
2 large oranges, peeled

Trim pork chops. Sprinkle both sides with salt and pepper. In a large skillet over medium-high heat, brown chops in butter or margarine. Pour off fat. Reduce heat to low.

continued on next page . . .

Pork Covington continued . . .

Meanwhile, in a small saucepan over low heat, stir orange juice, preserves, sherry, lemon rind and juice, mustard, ginger and dry mustard until preserves are melted. Thinly slice one orange and set aside for garnish. Dice remaining orange and add to sauce. Pour over browned chops, cover and simmer for 30 to 40 minutes or until chops are tender, basting several times.

To serve, arrange chops on a warm platter. Skim fat from sauce; spoon sauce over top of chops and garnish with orange slices. Pass remaining sauce separately. Makes 8 servings.

Carol A. Darstein
Orchard Park, NY

DANISH PUFF PORK CHOPS

"As a teenager, I first had this at the home of my mother's boss. I liked it so well, I kept the recipe until I was married to fix for my special guy! It's one of our favorites."

4 pork chops, ¾ to 1 inch thick	¼ cup all-purpose flour
2 tablespoons vegetable oil	1 cup milk
½ teaspoon salt	1 egg, lightly beaten
⅛ teaspoon pepper	1 small onion, grated
2 tablespoons butter or margarine	1 cup shredded sharp Cheddar cheese

Preheat oven to 350°. Trim fat from pork chops. In a 10-inch skillet over medium-high heat, brown chops on both sides in oil. Place in a shallow 2-quart baking dish. Sprinkle with salt and pepper; keep warm.

Meanwhile, in a small saucepan over medium heat, melt butter or margarine. Add flour. Cook and stir for 1 minute. Add milk. Stirring, bring to a boil and boil until thickened. Remove from heat. Beat in egg until smooth. Stir in onion and cheese. Over low heat, cook and stir just until cheese melts. Spoon one-fourth of the sauce over each chop, spreading to edges. Bake, uncovered, for 35 to 45 minutes or until chops are done and cheese is puffed and golden brown. Makes 4 servings.

Linda Liparuto Franklin
Roanoke, VA

SPICED POCKETS
(pictured on page 37)

¼ cup slivered almonds	⅛ teaspoon pepper
1 pound lean ground beef	6 pita bread rounds, 6 inches
1 cup chopped onion	each, slit
½ cup chili sauce	2 cups shredded iceberg
½ cup water	lettuce
¼ cup raisins	1½ cups shredded Monterey
½ teaspoon salt	Jack cheese
¼ teaspoon ground cinnamon	2 medium tomatoes, sliced
⅛ teaspoon ground cumin	

In a 10-inch skillet over medium-high heat, sauté almonds for 5 minutes or until toasted; set almonds aside. In same skillet, cook beef and onion until beef is no longer pink. Drain off fat. Add chili sauce, water, raisins, salt, cinnamon, cumin and pepper. Cook for 5 minutes or until liquid is evaporated, stirring occasionally. Stir in almonds.

Spoon one-sixth of the meat mixture into each pita. Serve with lettuce, cheese and tomatoes. Serve whole or cut in half. Makes 6 servings.

Janice E. Stewart
Salem, OR

CHINESE BEEF WITH CHEESE
(pictured on page 37)

"Guests love to watch this being put together. It looks beautiful and is economical, too."

1½ pounds beef round steak,	¼ cup vegetable oil
trimmed	2 bunches small green onions
2 tablespoons dry sherry	including tops, cut in
1 tablespoon cornstarch	1-inch pieces (1 cup)
¾ cup chili sauce	2 cloves garlic, crushed and
¼ cup soy sauce	minced
¼ cup light corn syrup	4 cups hot cooked rice
1 teaspoon ground ginger	1½ cups shredded Cheddar
¼ teaspoon crushed red	cheese
pepper	Additional green onions

continued on next page . . .

Chinese Beef with Cheese continued . . .

Slice meat into narrow strips, about 2 × ¼ inches; set aside.

In a medium bowl, stir sherry and cornstarch until smooth. Stir in chili sauce, soy sauce, corn syrup, ginger and red pepper; set aside.

In a wok or large skillet over high heat, heat 2 tablespoons of the oil. Add 1 cup green onions and garlic, stir-fry for 2 minutes or until green onions are limp. Using a slotted spoon, transfer to a second bowl. In wok or skillet, heat remaining 2 tablespoons oil. Add meat strips, stir-fry until meat loses its red color. Transfer to bowl with green onions. Reduce heat to medium. Stir sauce and pour into wok or skillet. Stirring, bring to a boil and boil for 1 minute. Return meat and onions to sauce, stir to coat and heat through. Serve immediately over rice, top with cheese and garnish with decoratively sliced green onions. Makes 4 generous servings.

Janice Elder
Spartanburg, SC

PEAR-SAUSAGE BREAKFAST BAKE

"This dish pleases even non-breakfast people. I make it ahead when house guests are coming, then re-heat in the morning. After our baby was born, my husband prepared this for our coming-home brunch."

1 can (16 oz.) pears, drained and ¼ cup syrup reserved	1 cup chopped walnuts
2 cups buttermilk baking mix	2 packages (8 oz. each) brown and serve sausages, cooked and drained
2 teaspoons ground cinnamon	
⅓ cup milk	¼ cup sugar
¼ cup vegetable oil	Warm maple syrup
2 eggs, lightly beaten	

Preheat oven to 400°. Lightly grease a shallow 2-quart baking dish. Dice pears; set aside.

Combine baking mix and 1 teaspoon of the cinnamon; set aside.

In a medium bowl, stir reserved pear syrup, milk, oil and eggs until well blended. Stir in baking mixture just until moistened. Gently stir in pears and nuts.

Arrange half of the sausages in baking dish. Carefully pour batter over. Arrange remaining sausages on top.

In a small bowl, combine sugar and remaining 1 teaspoon cinnamon. Sprinkle over sausages. Bake for 20 to 25 minutes or until a wooden pick inserted in center comes out clean.

Cut into squares and serve with syrup. Makes 10 servings.

Kathy Nelson
Vacaville, CA

BAHA'S MEXICAN BATTER MEATBALLS

(pictured on page 37)

"This has taco-flavored meatballs in a Yorkshire-type pudding — tender in center, crisp and crusty around edges. It's a good dish for a Mexican buffet."

1 slice white bread, torn in pieces	1½ pounds lean ground beef
¼ cup catsup	4 eggs
1 egg, lightly beaten	1½ cups milk
2 tablespoons water	3 tablespoons melted butter
1 envelope (1.37 oz.) dry onion soup mix	1½ cups all-purpose flour
1 tablespoon taco seasoning mix	1½ teaspoons baking powder
	1 teaspoon salt
1 tablespoon dried parsley flakes	1 can (4 oz.) diced green chilies, drained
⅛ teaspoon garlic powder	Cherry tomatoes (optional)
	Parsley (optional)
	Cheese sauce (optional)

Grease a 13×9×2-inch baking pan. In a large bowl, mix bread, catsup, 1 egg and water. Stir in onion soup mix, taco seasoning mix, parsley and garlic powder until well blended. Lightly mix in ground beef. Cover and refrigerate for 1 hour.

Preheat oven to 350°. Form mixture into twenty-four meatballs and place in four rows in baking pan.

In a small mixer bowl at medium speed, beat 4 eggs until foamy. At low speed, beat in milk and butter. Onto waxed paper, sift flour, baking powder and salt. Add all at once to egg mixture and beat at low speed until smooth. Stir in green chilies by hand. Pour evenly over meatballs. Bake for 45 to 50 minutes or until set and browned. Spoon off any accumulated fat before serving. If desired, garnish with tomatoes and parsley and serve with cheese sauce. Makes 8 servings.

Kathy Pickett
Yelm, WA

Kathy Pickett

Poultry and Other Entrées

SEAFOOD SUPPER STEW

"My father made me my first cookbook before I could read . . . he drew out everything in picture form. My mother taught me efficiency and how to taste, correct and create. When living on a sailboat for a year, I 'fine-tuned' many of my favorite recipes to be able to still produce delicious meals under adverse conditions. I have recently opened a small restaurant in our town . . . and I still love to cook, despite the 80-hour work weeks!"

1 cup sliced celery	½ teaspoon dried thyme
1 medium onion, chopped	leaves, crushed
2 cloves garlic, mashed	Dash of red pepper
2 tablespoons vegetable oil	2 ounces vermicelli or thin
1 can (14½ oz.) stewed	spaghetti, broken in
tomatoes	thirds
1 can (14½ oz.) clear chicken	1 pound halibut or turbot
broth	fillets, cut in 1-inch pieces
1 can (10¾ oz.) condensed	1 can (6½ oz.) chopped
tomato soup	clams, undrained
2 tablespoons chopped	1 package (6 oz.) frozen
parsley	cooked shrimp, thawed,
1 teaspoon dried basil leaves,	rinsed and drained
crushed	Salt and pepper (optional)
½ teaspoon dried rosemary	
leaves, crushed	

In a 5-quart Dutch oven over medium heat, sauté celery, onion and garlic in oil for 5 minutes or until onion is limp. Stir in stewed tomatoes, chicken broth, tomato soup, parsley, basil, rosemary, thyme and red pepper. Bring to a boil, stir in vermicelli or spaghetti; reduce heat to low, cover and simmer for 5 minutes or until almost tender. Add halibut or turbot, cover and simmer for 7 minutes or until fish flakes easily with a fork. Stir in clams with liquid and shrimp. Heat through. Season with salt and pepper to taste. Makes 4 (2-cup) servings.

Lia Azgapetian
Forest Falls, CA

Pictured on the preceding page, top to bottom, are Chicken Strudel with Mustard Sauce (see page 59) and Delightful Fish Fillets (see page 56).

CORN SALMON LOAF

"My grandmother raised her family of seven during the Depression and was good at recipes that were hearty and extended meat or fish. This freezes and reheats very well."

1 can (15½ oz.) salmon, drained	1 cup milk
2 cups cracker crumbs	2 eggs, beaten
1 can (17 oz.) cream-style corn	1 teaspoon salt
	⅛ teaspoon pepper
	1 tablespoon butter

Preheat oven to 400°. Grease an 8×8×2-inch baking dish. Remove bones and dark skin from salmon; flake.

In a large bowl, mix salmon, cracker crumbs, corn, milk, eggs, salt and pepper until well blended. Spread evenly in dish. Dot top with butter. Bake for 50 to 60 minutes or until a knife inserted in center comes out clean. Let cool for 5 minutes before serving. Makes 9 servings.

Pamela Laswell
Downey, CA

HERBED CHICKEN LIVERS

"This is a welcome substitute for steaks and roasts. Beef liver, cut in strips, can be substituted for the chicken livers."

1 medium onion, finely chopped	½ teaspoon dried oregano leaves, crushed
5 tablespoons butter or margarine	½ teaspoon salt
1 pound chicken livers	¼ teaspoon pepper
½ teaspoon dried parsley flakes, crushed	1½ cups dairy sour cream
½ teaspoon dried thyme leaves, crushed	¼ teaspoon lemon juice
	Hot cooked rice

In a 10-inch skillet over medium heat, sauté onion in butter or margarine for 5 minutes or until transparent. Add livers and brown on all sides. Sprinkle with herbs, salt and pepper. Cook and stir until livers are firm but still pink in the center or to desired doneness. Remove from heat. Stir in sour cream and lemon juice. Return to very low heat and, stirring constantly, heat through (do not boil). Serve over rice. Makes 6 servings.

Jeanne Bird
Cambridge, MA

CHICKEN SARONNO

6 skinless, boneless chicken breast halves	6 tablespoons butter or margarine
1 to 2 tablespoons curry powder	½ pound mushrooms, sliced
1 teaspoon salt	2 tablespoons lemon juice
¼ teaspoon pepper	2½ cups chicken broth
¼ teaspoon garlic powder	1 tablespoon cornstarch
All-purpose flour	Hot cooked rice
	Chopped tomato and parsley

Cut chicken into thin 1-inch strips. In a small bowl, mix curry powder, salt, pepper and garlic powder. Sprinkle over chicken; mix well. Toss seasoned chicken in flour to coat lightly. In a 5-quart Dutch oven over medium-high heat, brown chicken, half at a time, in 3 tablespoons of the butter or margarine, adding remaining butter or margarine as needed. Return chicken to pan. Add mushrooms and lemon juice.

In a small bowl, stir broth and cornstarch until well blended. Pour over chicken. Stirring constantly, bring to a boil; reduce heat to low, cover and simmer for 2 to 3 minutes or until chicken is cooked through.

Serve over rice; garnish with tomato and parsley. Makes 6 servings.

Leslie Bagley
West Jordan, UT

WILD RICE AND SHELLFISH

"I serve this in the center of a large platter with fresh green vegetables on either side and garnish with lemon slices and parsley. When fresh berries and melons are in season, I serve a fruit compote as a first course and add a light dessert such as a sorbet or mousse and cookies."

1 package (6 oz.) seasoned long grain and wild rice mix	1½ teaspoons dried basil leaves, crushed
1 large clove garlic, minced	½ pound sea scallops*
½ cup butter or margarine	½ pound medium shrimp, shelled and deveined*
½ pound mushrooms, sliced	¼ cup dry white wine

Prepare rice mix according to package directions, cooking until rice is tender and liquid is absorbed. Keep hot.

continued on next page . . .

Wild Rice and Shellfish continued . . .

Meanwhile, in a large skillet over medium-high heat, sauté garlic in butter or margarine for 30 seconds. Add mushrooms and basil, sauté for 2 minutes. Reduce heat to medium. Add scallops, cook and stir for 3 minutes. Add shrimp, cook and stir 3 minutes longer or until opaque and tender. Do not overcook. Add wine. Stir in hot rice and toss lightly to mix. Serve immediately. Makes 4 to 6 servings.

*Cut large scallops in bite-size pieces. If using frozen seafood, thaw, rinse and dry.

Gaye Klupenger
Portland, OR

CRAZY THREE-CHEESE PIZZA

"A very meaty dish with a chewy top. Makes a good party dish."

1 **pound lean ground beef**	½ **teaspoon dried oregano**
½ **pound bulk pork sausage**	**leaves, crushed**
1 **medium onion, chopped**	½ **teaspoon fennel seeds**
1 **teaspoon Worcestershire**	½ **teaspoon chili powder**
sauce	10 **ounces mozzarella cheese,**
1 **teaspoon soy sauce**	**thinly sliced**
1 **can (15 oz.) tomato sauce**	1 **cup all-purpose flour**
1 **medium green pepper,**	1 **cup milk**
chopped	2 **eggs**
1 **can (3.5 oz.) sliced**	1 **tablespoon vegetable oil**
mushrooms, drained	½ **teaspoon salt**
2 **tablespoons all-purpose**	¼ **cup grated Parmesan**
flour	**cheese**
½ **teaspoon dried Italian herb**	2 **tablespoons grated**
seasoning, crushed	**Romano cheese**

Preheat oven to 425°. In a large skillet over medium-high heat, sauté ground beef, sausage, onion, Worcestershire and soy sauce until meat is no longer pink; drain off fat. Stir in tomato sauce, green pepper, mushrooms, 2 tablespoons flour, herb seasoning, oregano, fennel seeds and chili powder. Stirring, bring to a boil and boil for 1 minute. Pour into an ungreased 13×9×2-inch baking pan. Top with mozzarella cheese.

In a small mixer bowl at medium speed, beat 1 cup flour, milk, eggs, oil and salt until smooth. Pour over mixture in pan; sprinkle with Parmesan and Romano cheese. Bake for 20 to 25 minutes or until golden brown. Let stand for 5 minutes before serving. Makes 12 (3-inch) servings.

Vickie Haney
Amarillo, TX

CHICKEN SUPREME

"Now that I'm retired from nursing, I have time to spend in my kitchen. I like feeding guests and sharing my recipes with my friends."

5 pounds chicken pieces	1 cup chopped celery
6 cups water	4 eggs, lightly beaten
1 onion, coarsely chopped	1 small onion, chopped
1 large bay leaf	1 jar (4 oz.) chopped
2 cups fresh bread crumbs,	pimiento, undrained
toasted	2 teaspoons salt
2 cups cooked rice	

In a 5-quart Dutch oven over high heat, bring chicken, water, coarsely chopped onion and bay leaf to a boil; reduce heat to low, cover and simmer for 1 hour or until chicken is tender. Remove chicken. Strain broth; skim fat from surface and set broth aside. When chicken is cool enough to handle, remove meat from bones; cut into bite-size pieces. You should have about 4 cups of meat. Discard bones and skin.

Preheat oven to 400°. In a large bowl, mix chicken, bread crumbs, rice, celery, eggs, remaining chopped onion, pimiento, salt and 3 cups of the reserved chicken broth. Pour into a shallow 3-quart baking dish. Bake for 25 to 30 minutes or until set. Cut into squares. Serve plain or use leftover chicken broth to make your favorite chicken gravy or mushroom sauce. Makes 10 to 12 servings.

Mrs. Ruth N. Sechrest
Umatilla, FL

Mrs. Ruth N. Sechrest

CHICKEN AND VEGETABLE CASSEROLE

"This dish has a crunchy topping with tender-crisp vegetables and chicken in a cream sauce. The main appeal to us is that the vegetables are not overcooked."

½ cup thinly sliced carrot	1 cup dairy sour cream
3 cups zucchini or summer	1 teaspoon salt
squash, cut in ½-inch	⅛ teaspoon pepper
cubes	1½ cups cubed cooked chicken
¼ cup butter or margarine	1 cup thinly sliced celery
¼ cup all-purpose flour	1 cup sliced mushrooms
1 cup milk	⅔ cup finely chopped onion
1½ cups herb-flavored stuffing	Freshly grated nutmeg
mix	(optional)

continued on next page . . .

Chicken and Vegetable Casserole continued . . .

Preheat oven to 350°. Grease a shallow 1½-quart baking dish. In a 3-quart saucepan over medium heat, cook carrot in boiling unsalted water for 5 minutes. Add squash and cook 5 minutes longer or until crisp-tender. Drain in a colander; set aside. In the same 3-quart saucepan over medium heat, melt butter or margarine. Stir in flour. Cook and stir for 1 to 2 minutes. Add milk. Stirring, bring to a boil and boil until thickened. Remove from heat. Stir in 1 cup of the stuffing mix, sour cream, salt and pepper. Gently stir in chicken, carrot, squash, celery, mushrooms and onion until blended. Transfer to baking dish. Sprinkle top with nutmeg and remaining ½ cup stuffing mix. Bake for 25 minutes or until mixture is bubbly and the top is lightly toasted. Makes 4 (1½-cup) servings.

Mrs. Gordon F. Mead
South Charleston, WV

SWISS CHICKEN CUTLETS

"Another version is to place a slice of Swiss cheese over each breast and then add remaining sauce. This is a little more like Veal Parmesan."

10	skinless, boneless chicken breast halves	¼	cup all-purpose flour
	Salt	2½	cups milk
2	eggs, beaten	½	teaspoon salt
1	cup dried bread crumbs	⅛	teaspoon pepper
¼	cup vegetable oil	½	cup dry white wine
3	tablespoons margarine	1	cup shredded Swiss cheese (4 oz.)

Place one chicken breast half between two pieces of waxed paper. Flatten to ¼-inch thickness with a wooden mallet or a rolling pin. Peel off waxed paper. Sprinkle lightly with salt. Dip both sides in egg, coat with crumbs; set aside. Repeat with remaining chicken pieces. In a large skillet over medium-high heat, brown chicken, a few pieces at a time, in oil for 2 minutes on each side or until lightly browned.

In a 2-quart saucepan over medium heat, melt margarine. Stir in flour. Cook and stir for 1 to 2 minutes. Add milk, salt and pepper. Stirring, bring to a boil and boil until thickened. Stir in wine. Remove from heat.

In a shallow 2½-quart baking dish, spread half of the sauce. Arrange chicken in dish and top with remaining sauce. Cover and refrigerate up to 24 hours if desired.

Bake, covered, in a preheated 350° oven for 20 minutes. Sprinkle cheese over top and bake, uncovered, 10 minutes longer or until cheese is melted and sauce is bubbly. Makes 10 servings.

Lois M. Kimble
Fort Worth, TX

HENNY PENNY CASSEROLE

"Henny Penny is my first recipe creation. No special garnishes are needed although if I have a fresh mushroom, I put it in the center after adding the soup."

1 medium onion, diced	1 teaspoon dried sage
1 tablespoon butter or	leaves, crushed
margarine	⅛ teaspoon garlic salt
1 cup sliced mushrooms	⅛ teaspoon pepper
2 cups cubed cooked chicken	1 can (10¾ oz.) condensed
or turkey	cream of chicken soup
2 cups soft bread crumbs	¼ teaspoon dried parsley
1 cup frozen peas, partially	flakes
thawed	⅛ teaspoon paprika
2 large eggs, lightly beaten	

Preheat oven to 350°. Grease a 1½-quart baking dish. In a 10-inch skillet over medium heat, sauté onion in butter or margarine for 6 minutes or until golden. Add mushrooms and sauté for 2 minutes.

In a large bowl, combine onion and mushrooms with chicken or turkey, bread crumbs, peas, eggs, sage, garlic salt and pepper, tossing lightly until mixed. Transfer to baking dish. Cover loosely with foil and bake for 40 minutes. Remove foil. Spread top with soup and sprinkle with parsley and paprika. Bake, uncovered, 20 minutes longer or until lightly browned. Makes 4 to 6 servings.

Barbara Winters-Shally
Aurora, CO

DELIGHTFUL FISH FILLETS

(pictured on page 49)

"My husband catches calico bass and fillets them beautifully. We eat fish at least three times a week in the summer, and I use this recipe of mine frequently. I always serve it with rice and green beans."

1 cup all-purpose flour*	5 tablespoons vegetable oil
1 teaspoon grated Parmesan	2 tablespoons butter or
cheese	margarine
½ teaspoon salt	Hot seasoned rice
⅛ teaspoon pepper	2 to 4 tablespoons lemon
½ cup milk	juice
2 eggs, beaten	2 to 4 tablespoons dry sherry
1½ pounds cod or sole fillets,	2 teaspoons chopped parsley
thawed and patted dry if	2 oranges, peeled and thinly
frozen	sliced

continued on next page . . .

Delightful Fish Fillets continued . . .

In a small shallow bowl, mix flour, cheese, salt and pepper.

In a second small shallow bowl, mix milk and eggs until smooth.

Roll fish in flour mixture, then in egg mixture and back in flour mixture.

In a large skillet over medium-high heat, fry fish in oil and butter or margarine for 5 minutes or until golden brown, turning once. (Reduce heat if browning too quickly.) Arrange fish on rice on a warm platter. Remove skillet from heat.

In a small bowl, mix lemon juice, sherry and parsley. Pour into skillet. Over medium-high heat, stir to loosen any browned bits clinging to the skillet and heat through.

Arrange orange slices on fish. Pour sauce over fish and serve immediately. Makes 6 servings.

*For a heavier, crispier coating, use fine dry bread crumbs instead of flour.

Mary Dinneen
Bristol, CT

CITRUS FRUITATTA

"Always gets compliments because it is so attractive and tasty . . . a new way to serve fruit and really a nice accompaniment for brunch menus."

1 **small pear, peeled and diced**	2 **medium oranges, sectioned and well drained (about ¾ cup)**
⅓ **cup chopped pitted dates**	
8 **eggs**	1 **small grapefruit, sectioned and well drained (about ½ cup)**
½ **cup milk**	
½ **teaspoon grated orange rind**	**Powdered sugar (optional)**
¼ **teaspoon salt**	

Preheat oven to 350°. Generously butter an 8½ × 1½-inch quiche dish. Evenly distribute pear and dates in dish. In a medium bowl, beat eggs, milk, orange rind and salt until well blended. Pour into quiche dish. Bake for 10 minutes. Arrange orange and grapefruit sections over egg mixture. Bake 20 to 25 minutes longer or until set. Let stand for 5 minutes before serving. Sprinkle with powdered sugar; cut in wedges. Makes 6 to 8 servings.

Paulette Williamson
Orlando, FL

PASTA FLORENTINE

"The food in Italy is so varied that it teases one into inventing an original dish. I serve this for dinner with Italian bread and an all-green salad such as a mixture of torn Romaine, endive, iceberg lettuce and a light oil and vinegar dressing."

1 package (10 oz.) frozen leaf spinach	¼ to ½ teaspoon freshly grated nutmeg
2 cups water	½ teaspoon garlic salt
2 slices lemon	8 ounces linguini, cooked and drained
1 bay leaf	Freshly ground pepper
12 ounces bay scallops*	Additional grated Parmesan cheese (optional)
1 can (5.33 oz.) evaporated milk	
1 large egg	
½ cup freshly grated Parmesan cheese	

Cook spinach according to package directions. Drain and squeeze dry; set aside.

In a small saucepan over high heat, bring water, lemon and bay leaf to a boil; reduce heat to low and simmer for 10 minutes. Increase heat to medium; add scallops. Bring to a boil; cover and simmer for 2 to 3 minutes or until scallops are opaque and tender. Remove bay leaf. Drain, set aside and keep warm.

In a small bowl, beat evaporated milk and egg slightly. Beat in ½ cup Parmesan cheese, nutmeg and garlic salt until combined. Separate spinach leaves. In a large saucepan over low heat, gently toss together linguini, spinach and egg mixture until egg has set and sauce has thickened slightly.

Place on a large heated platter. Sprinkle with pepper and top with scallops. Serve immediately and pass additional Parmesan cheese. Makes 4 (about 1-cup) servings.

*If using sea scallops, cut in bite-size pieces.

Lynn Blayney
Charlotte, NC

CHICKEN STRUDEL WITH MUSTARD SAUCE

(pictured on page 49)

"Very elegant for special dinners. The delicate, flaky crust encloses a creamy, tangy chicken mixture."

¼ cup unsalted butter
6 skinless, boneless chicken breast halves, cut in bite-size pieces
½ teaspoon salt
⅛ teaspoon pepper
½ cup Dijon mustard
1 pint whipping cream
1 tablespoon cornstarch (optional)

2 tablespoons water (optional)
7 phyllo pastry leaves (about 16 × 12 inches each)
¾ cup unsalted butter, melted
½ cup unseasoned toasted bread crumbs
1 egg
1 teaspoon water

In a large skillet over medium heat, melt ¼ cup butter. Add chicken, sprinkle with salt and pepper. Sauté until no longer pink (do not overcook). Transfer to a bowl; keep warm.

Add mustard to skillet and whisk in cream, blending well. Reduce heat to medium-low and simmer until thickened and reduced by one-fourth. Stir in juices from cooked chicken. If sauce is thin, dissolve cornstarch in 2 tablespoons water. Stir into sauce, bring to a boil and boil for 1 minute. Add chicken pieces and coat with sauce; set aside.

Preheat oven to 400°. Cover pastry leaves with a damp towel to prevent drying out. Place a 16-inch sheet of waxed paper on a second damp towel. Lay 1 leaf of phyllo on the waxed paper; brush generously with butter. Sprinkle with about 1 tablespoon of the bread crumbs. Repeat until all leaves are stacked; brushing butter on only the edges of the last leaf.

With a slotted spoon, remove chicken from sauce, draining slightly. Cover remaining sauce and keep warm. Spread chicken along one long side of pastry, leaving a 2-inch border on each end. Carefully fold edges over filling, fold up bottom edge. Using the towel and waxed paper, roll as for a jelly roll starting from long side covered with chicken. Place seam-side down on an ungreased baking sheet. With a sharp knife, score top of roll to mark six slices.

In a small bowl, beat egg with 1 teaspoon water. Carefully brush on top and sides of roll without dripping on the baking sheet. Brush with any remaining butter. Bake for 12 to 15 minutes or until crisp and golden brown. Loosen from baking sheet and slice with a sharp knife. If making ahead, reheat in a 300° oven for 15 to 20 minutes. Reheat sauce over low heat. Serve strudel with sauce. Makes 6 servings.

Ann N. Chupita
New Brighton, MN

SAUSAGE-STUFFED CHICKEN BREASTS

"This dish has the lightness of chicken with a bold influence. It's a family favorite and the only way I get my husband to eat chicken!"

8 large boneless chicken breast halves	1 teaspoon dried oregano leaves, crushed
1¼ pounds sweet Italian sausage, casings removed	1 teaspoon dried parsley leaves, crushed
1 jar (15 oz.) spaghetti sauce	½ teaspoon garlic powder
1 cup Italian-seasoned bread crumbs	⅓ cup water

Preheat oven to 375°. With a sharp knife, cut a pocket in the thickest part of each breast half; set aside.

In a large bowl, mix sausage, ½ cup of the spaghetti sauce, bread crumbs, oregano, parsley and garlic powder until blended. Stuff one-eighth of the mixture into each pocket; secure with a wooden pick. Place in a shallow 3-quart baking dish.

In a small bowl, mix remaining spaghetti sauce and water. Pour half of the mixture over chicken. Cover with foil. Bake for 35 minutes. Pour remaining sauce mixture over chicken. Bake, uncovered, 15 minutes longer. Spoon sauce over before serving. Makes 8 servings.

Linda Paladino
Beachwood, NJ

SAUTÉED SCALLOPS AND PEAS

"I made up this recipe one night when I was trying to decide how to serve a small amount of peas from my garden."

1 pound sea scallops, cut in bite-size pieces if large	1 cup peas, thawed if frozen
1 cup sliced mushrooms	½ teaspoon dried tarragon leaves, crushed
½ cup chopped green onion tops	¼ teaspoon salt
1 small clove garlic, minced	⅛ teaspoon pepper
3 tablespoons butter	Hot cooked wild rice

In a large skillet over medium heat, sauté scallops, mushrooms, green onion tops and garlic in butter for 10 minutes or until scallops are tender and opaque. Add peas, tarragon, salt and pepper. Sauté for 2 minutes or until peas are heated through. Serve immediately with rice. Makes 4 servings.

Barbara H. Howard
Taylor Mill, KY

Cakes and Cookies

SMOKY MOUNTAIN JAM CAKE

"For a higher cake I double the entire recipe and bake four layers. The jam between the layers gives it just the right delicate combination of flavors, we think."

2 cups all-purpose flour	½ teaspoon vanilla extract
½ teaspoon baking soda	¼ cup buttermilk
½ teaspoon ground cinnamon	½ cup strawberry preserves
½ teaspoon ground cloves	½ cup frozen whole straw-
½ teaspoon ground allspice	berries or blackberries,
¼ teaspoon salt	thawed and sliced
1 cup sugar	1 cup plum jam
¾ cup butter	Caramel Icing (see below)
3 eggs	

Preheat oven to 350°. Grease two 9×1½-inch round cake pans. Line with waxed paper; grease and flour waxed paper. In a medium bowl, combine flour, baking soda, cinnamon, cloves, allspice and salt; set aside.

In a large mixer bowl at medium speed, beat sugar and butter until creamy. Add eggs and vanilla and beat for 2 minutes or until well blended. At low speed, beat in flour mixture in two additions alternately with buttermilk, starting and ending with flour mixture, beating well after each addition. Beat in preserves and strawberries or blackberries until well mixed. Pour into pans. Bake for 35 to 45 minutes or until a wooden pick inserted in center comes out clean and cakes pull away from sides of pans. Cool in pans on wire racks for 10 minutes. Remove from pans; remove waxed paper immediately. Cool cakes completely.

Spread jam between layers. Frost top and sides with Caramel Icing. Makes 12 to 16 servings.

CARAMEL ICING

½ cup butter	¼ cup milk
1 cup packed brown sugar	2 cups powdered sugar

In a medium saucepan over medium heat, melt butter. Stir in brown sugar. Add milk. Stirring, bring to a full boil. Cool completely. With a wooden spoon, gradually beat in powdered sugar until of spreading consistency. Makes 2 cups.

Mrs. Phillip B. Stover
Burkesville, KY

Pictured on the preceding page, top to bottom, are Vegetarian Cake (see page 67), Piña Colada Cheesecake (see page 74), Ragalich (see page 64), and Hawaiian Macadamia Nut Bites (see page 66).

BUTTERSCOTCH TORTE

"I love to cook and bake, but I work full-time and don't have much time to spend in the kitchen. This dessert is light and airy, but rich. I've had many compliments on the recipe and am asked to bring it whenever I'm supposed to take something for a meal."

6 egg yolks	1 cup finely chopped pecans
1½ cups sugar	6 egg whites
2 teaspoons vanilla extract	2 cups whipped topping
1 teaspoon almond extract	Butterscotch Sauce (see
½ teaspoon baking powder	below)
2 cups graham cracker	
crumbs	

Preheat oven to 350°. Grease two 9 × 1½-inch round cake pans. Line with waxed paper and grease and flour the paper. In a large mixer bowl at medium speed, beat egg yolks for 2 minutes. At low speed, slowly add sugar, vanilla and almond extracts, and baking powder. Beat until well blended. Stir in graham cracker crumbs and nuts.

In a small mixer bowl at high speed, beat egg whites until stiff peaks form. By hand, gently stir about one-third of the egg whites into the egg yolk mixture to lighten. Fold in remaining egg whites. Spread evenly in pans. Bake for 30 to 40 minutes or until a wooden pick inserted in center comes out clean and top is set. Cool in pans on wire racks for 5 minutes. Loosen edges of cakes from pans with a knife and remove cakes from pans; remove waxed paper immediately. Cool layers completely on wire racks.

Spread 1 cup of the whipped topping between layers and spread remaining topping on top of cake to within ½ inch of edge. Drizzle sauce over top and down sides of cake. Serve immediately or refrigerate until 1 hour before serving. Makes 18 servings.

BUTTERSCOTCH SAUCE

1 cup packed brown sugar	¼ cup water
1 tablespoon all-purpose	1 egg, lightly beaten
flour	½ teaspoon vanilla extract
¼ cup orange juice	¼ cup butter

While cake is baking, in a small saucepan, mix brown sugar and flour. Stir in orange juice, water, egg and vanilla until smooth. Add butter. Stirring over medium heat, bring to a boil and boil for 3 minutes or until thick and shiny. Cool. Makes about 1½ cups.

Carolyn Clear
Flora, IN

Carolyn Clear

ORANGE-PECAN ICEBOX COOKIES

"My grandmother made icebox cookies almost exclusively, and I am fortunate to have her recipes. I have a full-time career and many hobbies, but still am old-fashioned in that I prefer to prepare all my food from scratch. I like recipes that adapt to my life-style — like these cookies that can be made up, kept in the refrigerator and baked fresh when needed."

½ cup sugar	1 tablespoon grated orange
½ cup packed brown sugar	rind
½ cup butter or margarine,	2 tablespoons orange juice
softened	2 cups whole wheat or all-
½ cup solid vegetable	purpose flour
shortening	½ teaspoon baking soda
1 egg	½ cup chopped pecans

In a large mixer bowl at medium speed, beat sugar, brown sugar, butter or margarine, and shortening until light and fluffy. Beat in egg, orange rind and juice. At low speed, gradually beat in flour and baking soda until moistened. Beat in pecans (mixture will be soft). Divide into three portions; place each on waxed paper and form into a 1 ½-inch diameter roll, about 8 inches long. Wrap each portion in the waxed paper then in foil and chill overnight or up to several days.

Preheat oven to 350°. Grease baking sheets. Unwrap rolls of dough and slice ¼ inch thick. Place 1 inch apart on baking sheets. Bake for 8 to 10 minutes or until golden. Cool cookies on wire racks.

Store in an airtight container. Dough keeps in the refrigerator up to 1 week. Makes about 6 dozen.

Ann Cott
Pueblo, CO

RAGALICH (Raspberry Pinwheels)

(pictured on page 61)

1 cup butter or margarine,	⅛ teaspoon salt
softened	2 ¾ cups all-purpose flour
1 package (8 oz.) cream	½ cup red raspberry preserves
cheese, softened	½ cup finely chopped walnuts
½ cup sugar	Sugar
2 teaspoons vanilla extract	

In a large mixer bowl at medium speed, beat butter or margarine and cream cheese until light and fluffy. Beat in ½ cup sugar, vanilla and salt until blended. At low speed, gradually beat in flour until well mixed and mixture forms a ball. Divide dough into two portions. Wrap each in waxed paper and chill for 30 minutes.

continued on next page . . .

Ragalich continued . . .

Preheat oven to 350°. Lightly grease baking sheets. On a lightly floured surface, roll one portion of dough at a time to ¼-inch thickness, forming a 14 × 10-inch rectangle. Spread each with ¼ cup of the preserves, sprinkle with ¼ cup of the walnuts. Roll as for a jelly roll, starting from the long side. With a sharp knife, cut ½-inch slices. Dip one cut side in sugar. Place, sugar-side up, 1 inch apart on baking sheets. Bake for 25 to 30 minutes or until golden brown. Cool cookies on wire racks.

Store in an airtight container. Makes 4½ dozen.

Phyllis Hlavin
California

CHOCOLATE MOUSSE CAKE

"This dessert is for special occasions. It has a luscious creamy filling and topping. I love to cook and collect recipes and cookbooks. My specialty is Italian food which is a part of my heritage."

7 ounces semisweet chocolate	1 cup sugar
½ cup butter	7 egg yolks
7 egg whites, at room temperature	2 teaspoons vanilla extract
⅛ teaspoon cream of tartar	2 cups whipping cream
	½ cup powdered sugar

Preheat oven to 325°. Grease a 9-inch springform pan. In a small saucepan over low heat, melt chocolate and butter. Remove from heat; set aside.

In a large mixer bowl at high speed, beat egg whites and cream of tartar until very stiff. Beat in 4 tablespoons of the sugar, 1 tablespoon at a time, until sugar is dissolved; set aside.

Without washing beaters, in a small mixer bowl at medium-high speed, beat egg yolks and remaining ¾ cup sugar for 2 minutes or until thick and pale yellow. At low speed, gradually beat in chocolate mixture and 1 teaspoon of the vanilla until blended. Stir one-third of the egg whites into chocolate mixture. Carefully fold batter into remaining whites. Pour about three-fourths of the batter into springform pan. (Cover the remaining batter and refrigerate.) Bake cake for 35 to 40 minutes or until dry and a knife inserted in center comes out clean. Cool in pan on a wire rack. (Center of cake will fall.)

In a small mixer bowl at medium speed, beat cream, powdered sugar and remaining 1 teaspoon vanilla until stiff peaks form.

Remove outer rim of cake pan; place cake with metal base on a serving plate. Fill center of cake with refrigerated mousse. Frost top and sides with whipped cream frosting. Chill for 2 hours or up to 12 hours before serving. Decorate with grated chocolate if desired. Makes 12 servings.

Joanne Nawrocki
Lafayette, CO

BIZCOCHOS DE VINO (Spanish Wine Cookies)

"After I married and moved to Texas in 1954, my mother-in-law showed me how to prepare many Mexican dishes. These cookies are popular here on the border for weddings and holidays."

½ pound lard, at room temperature	½ cup rosé wine
½ cup sugar	½ cup sugar
1 egg yolk	1½ teaspoons ground cinnamon
2½ cups all-purpose flour	

Preheat oven to 350°. Lightly grease baking sheets. In a large mixer bowl at medium speed, beat lard and ½ cup sugar until light and fluffy. Beat in egg yolk. At low speed, beat in flour in three additions alternately with wine, starting and ending with flour, beating well after each addition (mixture will be soft). Chill for 30 minutes. Divide into four portions. On a well floured surface, roll one portion of dough at a time to ¼-inch thickness. With a sharp knife or a pastry cutter with a decorative edge, cut 2-inch triangles.

In a small bowl, mix ½ cup sugar and cinnamon. Dip each triangle completely in sugar mixture and place on baking sheets. Bake for 12 to 15 minutes or until lightly browned. While warm, coat each triangle again with sugar mixture, then cool on wire racks. Store in an airtight container. Makes about 5 dozen.

Agnes H. Humphrey
El Paso, TX

Agnes H. Humphrey

HAWAIIAN MACADAMIA NUT BITES

(pictured on page 61)

"I make these for the holidays and include them in my Christmas cookie assortments that I give as gifts. Well worth the price of macadamia nuts!"

½ cup butter or margarine, softened	1 can (5 oz.) whole macadamia nuts (about 1 cup)
½ cup sugar	¼ cup semisweet chocolate chips
1 egg	
1 tablespoon vanilla extract	1 teaspoon solid vegetable shortening
1½ cups all-purpose flour	
⅛ teaspoon salt	

Preheat oven to 350°. In a large mixer bowl at low speed, beat butter or margarine and sugar until blended. Increase speed to medium-high, beat until fluffy. Beat in egg and vanilla. At low speed, beat in flour and salt. Shape 1 teaspoon of dough around each macadamia nut. Place on ungreased baking sheets. Bake for 10 to 13 minutes or until golden around base of each cookie. Cool cookies on wire racks.

continued on next page . . .

Hawaiian Macadamia Nut Bites continued . . .

In a small saucepan over low heat, melt chocolate chips and shortening. With a spoon, drizzle over cookies. Store in a tightly covered container. Makes 5½ dozen.

Mary Anne McFaul
Castro Valley, CA

VEGETARIAN CAKE

(pictured on page 61)

"This recipe was handed down from my mother. I serve it at Christmas time since my family does not care for traditional fruitcake."

2 cups all-purpose flour	¾ cup currants
3 teaspoons baking powder	¾ cup raisins
1½ teaspoons ground cinnamon	¾ cup chopped walnuts
1½ teaspoons ground allspice	1 tablespoon grated orange peel
¾ teaspoon baking soda	1½ cups packed brown sugar
¼ teaspoon salt	¾ cup butter or margarine, softened
1½ cups peeled, shredded apples (about 2 medium)	3 eggs
1½ cups peeled, shredded carrots (about 3 medium)	2 tablespoons light molasses
1½ cups peeled, shredded potatoes (about 2 medium)	

Preheat oven to 350°. Generously grease and flour a 10-inch fluted tube pan. Onto waxed paper, sift flour, baking powder, cinnamon, allspice, baking soda and salt; set aside.

In a medium bowl, gently toss apples, carrots, potatoes, currants, raisins, nuts and orange peel; set aside.

In a large mixer bowl at medium speed, beat brown sugar and butter or margarine until fluffy. Add eggs and molasses and beat until well blended. At low speed, beat in dry ingredients until moistened. Gradually add vegetable mixture and beat until well blended. Spoon into pan. Bake for 60 minutes or until a wooden pick inserted 1 inch from outer edge comes out clean and cake pulls away from pan. Cool on a wire rack for 10 minutes; remove cake from pan and cool completely.

Cover and store in the refrigerator. Best served the second day. Slice with a sharp knife. Makes 12 to 16 servings.

Note: If desired, just before serving, drizzle with Powdered Sugar Glaze (see page 24). Decorate with red and green candied cherries.

Dorothy Snover
Pensacola, FL

BREAKFAST COOKIES

⅓ cup whole bran cereal
¼ cup orange juice
1 cup all-purpose or whole wheat flour
1 cup quick-cooking oats
⅓ cup dry milk powder
1 teaspoon baking powder
½ teaspoon baking soda
½ teaspoon salt
¼ cup butter or margarine, softened

¼ cup packed brown sugar
1 large egg
¼ cup honey
1½ teaspoons vanilla extract
1½ teaspoons grated orange rind
½ teaspoon grated lemon rind
1 cup finely chopped pecans
½ cup raisins
½ cup finely chopped dates

Preheat oven to 375°. Grease baking sheets. In a small bowl, stir bran cereal and orange juice; set aside for 5 minutes.

In a medium bowl, combine flour, oats, milk powder, baking powder, baking soda and salt; set aside.

In a large mixer bowl at medium speed, beat butter or margarine and brown sugar until light and fluffy. Beat in egg until well blended. Add bran cereal mixture, honey, vanilla, orange and lemon rind; beat until blended. At low speed, beat in flour mixture until moistened. Stir in pecans, raisins and dates. Drop by tablespoonfuls onto baking sheets, about 1½ inches apart. Bake for 10 to 12 minutes or until medium brown. Cool cookies on wire racks.

Store in an airtight container. Makes 3 to 4 dozen.

Shirley A. Blackwell
Fulton, MD

TROPICAL HONEY CAKE

"Although my home is in Richmond, I am presently living in Germany. I serve this cake for breakfast and with tea. It has been sold at bazaars and bake sales and everyone likes it."

½ cup quick-cooking oats
½ cup packed brown sugar
3 tablespoons all-purpose flour
¼ cup cold butter
3 eggs
1½ cups all-purpose flour
1¼ cups honey
1 cup whole wheat flour
1 cup vegetable oil
1 teaspoon salt

1 teaspoon ground cinnamon
1 teaspoon baking soda
1 teaspoon almond extract
1 can (8 oz.) crushed pineapple in its own juice, well drained
½ cup chopped walnuts
¼ cup flaked coconut
1 can (11 oz.) mandarin orange segments, well drained

continued on next page . . .

Tropical Honey Cake continued . . .

Preheat oven to 350°. Grease a 13×9×2-inch baking pan. In a medium bowl, mix oats, brown sugar and 3 tablespoons all-purpose flour. With a pastry blender or two knives, cut in butter until pieces are the size of small peas; set aside.

In a large mixer bowl at low speed, beat eggs. Add 1½ cups all-purpose flour, honey, whole wheat flour, oil, salt, cinnamon, baking soda and almond extract; beat until well blended. By hand, stir in pineapple, nuts and coconut. Gently stir in oranges. Pour into pan. Sprinkle streusel over top. Bake for 45 to 50 minutes or until a wooden pick inserted in center comes out clean and cake starts to pull away from pan. Makes 24 (2×2-inch) servings.

Note: For a dessert cake, add 6 ounces butterscotch or chocolate chips to the cake batter.

Carolyn Lucas
Richmond, VA

WALNUT SQUARES

"I serve this mainly during the holidays on my cookie tray. It has been a favorite of my family and friends for the last twenty-five years. I also cut it into larger squares and serve with a fork as a dessert."

2 cups all-purpose flour	1 tablespoon water
½ teaspoon salt	1 teaspoon vanilla extract
1 cup solid vegetable shortening	1 package (6 oz.) semisweet chocolate chips
½ cup sugar	2 egg whites
1½ cups packed brown sugar	¾ cup ground walnuts
2 egg yolks	

Preheat oven to 375°. Grease a 15½ × 10½ × 1-inch jelly roll pan. In a small bowl, mix flour and salt; set aside.

In a large mixer bowl at medium speed, beat shortening until creamy. Gradually beat in sugar and ½ cup of the brown sugar. Add egg yolks and continue beating until light and fluffy. Beat in water and vanilla. Add flour mixture and beat until well blended. Spread batter evenly in pan. Sprinkle with chocolate chips.

In a small mixer bowl at high speed, beat egg whites until soft peaks form. Reduce speed to low and gradually beat in remaining 1 cup brown sugar. Increase speed to high and beat until fluffy. With a metal spatula, spread egg white mixture over chocolate chips; sprinkle with walnuts and pat lightly into meringue. Bake for 20 minutes or until meringue is set and dry on top. Cool in pan on a wire rack at least 2 hours.

Cut into 1½-inch squares. Best served same day. Lightly cover leftovers and store in a cool place. Makes 70 (1½ inches each).

Mrs. Mary Newman
Glenview, IL

FANCY CHOCOLATE NUT CAKE

"I received this recipe from an old Czechoslovakian lady and adapted it to suit American measures and convenience. There are no shortcuts in making the recipe, but the results are worthwhile. I garnish the top with a nut on each wedge."

1 cup butter, softened	1½ teaspoons vanilla extract
1½ cups powdered sugar	8 large egg whites
8 large egg yolks	Chocolate Filling (see below)
2 cups finely ground walnuts or blanched almonds	Chocolate Glaze (see page 71)
1 package (6 oz.) semisweet chocolate chips, melted and cooled	16 walnut halves or blanched almonds
3½ tablespoons all-purpose flour	

Preheat oven to 350°. Grease three 9×1½-inch round cake pans. Line with waxed paper, grease and flour the paper. In a large mixer bowl at medium-high speed, beat butter for 2 minutes or until light and fluffy. Very slowly add powdered sugar and beat 2 minutes longer or until blended.

In a small mixer bowl at medium-high speed, beat egg yolks for 2 minutes or until thick and pale yellow. Add to butter mixture and beat until blended, scraping sides of bowl as needed. Beat in nuts, chocolate and flour. Add vanilla and beat until well blended.

In a clean large mixer bowl at high speed, beat egg whites until stiff but not dry. Stir one-third of the egg whites into chocolate mixture to lighten. Carefully fold remaining whites into batter. Pour into pans. Bake for 30 to 35 minutes or until cakes pull away from sides of pans. Cool in pans on wire racks for 5 minutes. Remove cakes from pans; remove waxed paper immediately. Cool cakes completely on wire racks.

To assemble, place one layer of cake on a serving plate and spread with half of the filling. Top with a second cake layer and spread with remaining filling. Top with remaining cake layer. Cover top and sides of cake with warm glaze. Decorate cake with nuts. Serve or cover and refrigerate until 2 hours before serving. Makes 16 servings.

CHOCOLATE FILLING

⅓ cup semisweet chocolate chips	½ cup milk
2 cups ground walnuts or blanched almonds	⅓ cup sugar
	¼ cup butter
	1 tablespoon rum

In a small saucepan over low heat, melt chocolate chips. Add nuts, milk and sugar. Stirring constantly, cook over medium heat until very thick. Remove from heat. Add butter and stir until melted. Stir in rum. Cool completely.

Use as a filling for Fancy Chocolate Nut Cake or in cake of your choice. Makes about 2 cups.

CHOCOLATE GLAZE

1 package (6 oz.) semisweet chocolate chips	3 tablespoons milk
2 tablespoons butter	2 tablespoons light corn syrup

In a small saucepan over low heat, melt chocolate chips and butter. Remove from heat; stir in milk and corn syrup. Beat until smooth and glossy. Spread warm glaze over cooled cake. (This glaze is very thin.) Makes about 1 cup.

Mary L. Butler
St. Paul, MN

Mary L. Butler

CHOCOLATE WALNUT FRUITCAKE

"We are real chocolate lovers, and this recipe has been a hit with my family for many years. Wrapped well, it will keep for months in the refrigerator."

2 cups all-purpose flour	¼ cup butter or margarine, melted
1½ cups sugar	2 cups diced candied fruit
½ cup unsweetened cocoa powder	1½ cups coarsely chopped walnuts
1 teaspoon baking soda*	1 cup thinly sliced pitted dates
1 teaspoon salt	1 cup raisins
1 cup dairy sour cream	
2 eggs	
1 teaspoon vanilla extract	

Preheat oven to 300°. Place a baking pan half full of warm water on lowest rack of oven. Generously grease and flour a 9-inch tube pan. Onto waxed paper, sift flour, sugar, cocoa powder, baking soda and salt; set aside.

In a large mixer bowl at medium speed, beat sour cream, eggs and vanilla until blended. Add butter or margarine and beat until blended. At low speed, gradually beat in flour mixture until blended; beat at medium speed for 2 minutes. By hand, stir in candied fruit, nuts, dates and raisins until well blended. Spoon into pan. Bake in center of oven for 1¾ hours to 2 hours or until a wooden pick inserted 2 inches from outer edge comes out clean. Cool in pan on a wire rack for 20 minutes; remove cake from pan and cool completely on wire rack.

Wrap with plastic wrap, then with foil. Store in the refrigerator for 1 week before serving. Slice with a sharp knife. Makes 1.

*At altitudes above 5,000 feet, use only ¾ teaspoon baking soda.

Georgiann Jensen
Waynesville, MO

Georgiann Jensen

APRICOT BARS

"This recipe has been complimented highly anywhere I have taken these crunchy and chewy cookies. It is unique in that it is as good three or four days old as it is the day it is made. I hope you will enjoy it as much as we do. Absolutely delicious."

1 cup butter or margarine, softened	1½ cups finely chopped pecans or walnuts
1 cup sugar	1¼ cups apricot preserves
1 large egg	1 egg white, lightly beaten
Pinch of salt	Sugar
2½ cups all-purpose flour	

Preheat oven to 375°. Grease and flour a 13×9×2-inch baking pan. In a large mixer bowl at medium speed, beat butter or margarine until light and fluffy. Gradually beat in 1 cup sugar, egg and salt. At low speed, gradually beat in flour and nuts until moistened and well blended. Reserve 1½ cups of the mixture for topping. Pat remaining mixture into pan and press lightly. Evenly spread apricot preserves over dough.

Form reserved mixture into a ball. On a lightly floured surface, roll to ¼-inch thickness. Cut fifteen 2-inch circles and place on top of preserves. Crumble remaining pieces of dough around circles. Brush circles with egg white and sprinkle surface with sugar. Bake for 30 to 40 minutes or until medium brown and top is crisped. Cool pan on a wire rack. While slightly warm, cut into 30 small bars or 15 squares. Cover and store in a cool place. Makes 30 (3×1¼-inch) bars or 15 squares.

Mary L. Drace
Amarillo, TX

SESAME SEED COOKIES

"This is my blue ribbon recipe. My family calls it this because every time I've entered it into a fair, I've won first prize. It's a really crisp, light cookie."

1 can (2.12 oz.) sesame seeds	½ teaspoon almond extract (optional)
1 cup sugar	2 cups sifted all-purpose flour
1 cup solid vegetable shortening	½ teaspoon baking soda
1 egg	½ teaspoon salt
1 teaspoon vanilla extract	

In a heavy 10-inch skillet or 3-quart saucepan over low heat, cook and stir sesame seeds for 5 minutes or just until lightly browned. Do not use oil. Transfer seeds to a bowl; set aside.

continued on next page . . .

Sesame Seed Cookies continued . . .

Preheat oven to 350°. In a large mixer bowl at low speed, beat sugar and shortening until blended. Increase speed to medium and beat until light and fluffy. Beat in egg, vanilla and almond extracts. At low speed, gradually beat in flour, baking soda and salt until blended. Add sesame seeds and mix well.

Drop by rounded teaspoonfuls onto ungreased baking sheets. Flatten tops slightly with tines of a fork. Bake for 12 to 15 minutes or until crisp and golden. Cool cookies on wire racks.

Store in an airtight container in a cool place. Makes 4 dozen.

Mary A. Izzo
Cottonwood, AZ

EASY CHOCOLATE CAKE BROWNIES

2 cups all-purpose flour	¼ cup unsweetened cocoa
2 cups sugar	powder
1 teaspoon baking soda	½ cup buttermilk or sour milk
1 teaspoon ground cinnamon	2 eggs
1 cup water	1 teaspoon vanilla extract
½ cup margarine	Topping (see below)

Preheat oven to 400°. Grease a 15½ × 10½ × 1-inch jelly roll pan. In a large bowl, stir flour, sugar, baking soda and cinnamon; set aside.

In a small saucepan over medium heat, cook and stir water, margarine and cocoa powder until margarine is melted; remove from heat and set aside. In a medium bowl, beat buttermilk or sour milk, eggs and vanilla until blended. Stir in chocolate mixture. Pour over dry ingredients and mix until smooth. Spread evenly in pan. Bake for 10 to 12 minutes or until a wooden pick inserted in center comes out clean. While brownies bake, make topping and spread on hot brownies. Cool. Store loosely covered in a cool place. Makes about 3 dozen.

TOPPING

½ cup margarine	1 box (1 lb.) powdered
5 tablespoons buttermilk or	sugar, sifted
sour milk	1 teaspoon vanilla extract
¼ cup unsweetened cocoa	1 cup chopped nuts
powder	

In a 2-quart saucepan over medium heat, cook and stir margarine, buttermilk or sour milk, and cocoa powder until margarine is melted and mixture boils. Remove from heat. Gradually stir in powdered sugar and vanilla until smooth. Add nuts and mix well. Makes 2¼ cups.

Mrs. Elizabeth Wilson
Santa Rosa, CA

OATMEAL CARAMEL DELIGHTS

32 light caramels
5 tablespoons half-and-half
¾ cup butter or margarine, melted
¾ cup packed brown sugar
1 cup all-purpose flour

½ teaspoon baking soda
¼ teaspoon salt
1 cup quick-cooking oats
1 package (6 oz.) semisweet chocolate chips
½ cup chopped pecans

Preheat oven to 350°. Grease a 12×8×2-inch baking dish. In a medium saucepan over low heat, melt caramels in half-and-half. Stir until smooth; set aside.

In a medium bowl, mix butter or margarine and brown sugar. Stir in flour, baking soda and salt. Stir in oats. Press half the mixture into the bottom of baking dish. Sprinkle with chocolate chips and nuts. Drizzle with caramel mixture. Sprinkle with remaining crumb mixture. Bake for 15 to 20 minutes or until golden brown. Cool baking dish on a wire rack. Chill at least 1 hour before cutting into 2×1½-inch pieces. Makes 32.

Barb Schlafer
Appleton, WI

PIÑA COLADA CHEESECAKE

(pictured on page 61)

1¼ cups fine graham cracker crumbs
⅓ cup flaked coconut
¼ cup finely chopped walnuts
⅓ cup butter, melted
2 packages (8 oz. each) cream cheese, softened
1 cup sugar

3 large eggs
1 tablespoon rum extract (optional)
1 teaspoon vanilla extract
¼ teaspoon salt
3 cups dairy sour cream
Pineapple topping
Shredded coconut (optional)

In a medium bowl, mix crumbs, flaked coconut and walnuts. Stir in butter until evenly moistened. Press mixture evenly against bottom and 1½ inches up sides of a 9×3-inch springform pan. Chill.

Preheat oven to 375°. In a large mixer bowl at medium speed, beat cream cheese until fluffy. Gradually beat in sugar. Add eggs, one at a time, scraping bowl and beaters occasionally. Add extracts and salt. At low speed, beat in sour cream until blended. Pour into crust and smooth the top. Bake for 1 hour or until top is set and golden brown. Cool to room temperature, away from drafts. Remove outer rim of pan. Chill.

To serve, spoon topping onto center of cake top and surround with a ring of coconut if desired. Makes 12 servings.

Lizabeth Schroeder
Roseville, CA

Pies and Pastries

DANISH APPLE BARS

"Best when served warm from the oven."

3 cups all-purpose flour	7 cups peeled, diced tart
1 teaspoon salt	cooking apples
1 cup solid vegetable	1 cup sugar
shortening	1 teaspoon ground cinnamon
7 tablespoons milk	1 egg white, lightly beaten
1 egg yolk	Vanilla Glaze (see below)
1 cup crushed corn flakes	

Preheat oven to 375°. Into a large bowl, sift flour and salt. With a pastry blender or two knives, cut in shortening until mixture resembles coarse crumbs. In a small bowl, beat milk and egg yolk until blended. Stir into crumb mixture until moistened. Divide into two equal portions.

On a lightly floured surface, roll one portion of dough into a 17 × 12-inch rectangle. Transfer to a 15½ × 10½ × 1-inch jelly roll pan, pressing dough up sides of pan. Sprinkle corn flakes in bottom.

In a large bowl, stir apples, sugar and cinnamon until well mixed. Spread evenly over corn flakes. Roll remaining dough into a rectangle, 1 inch larger than pan, and place on top of apples, pressing to seal edges. Pierce top with a fork to permit steam to escape during baking. Brush top with egg white. Bake for 50 to 60 minutes or until golden brown. Spread top with glaze while still warm.

Cut into 2 × 1-inch bars or 3-inch squares. Serve warm or at room temperature. Makes 75 bars or 15 squares.

VANILLA GLAZE

1 cup powdered sugar	1 teaspoon vanilla extract
2 tablespoons water	

In a small bowl, stir powdered sugar, water and vanilla until smooth. Makes about ½ cup.

Susan Immel
Baltic, OH

Pictured on the preceding page, top to bottom, are Blueberry Meringue Pie (see page 82), Lemon Sour Cream Tarts (see page 84), and Hungarian Kiffles (see page 80).

CHOCOLATE BANANA CREAM PIE

"I developed this crust to use instead of the usual pastry. It stays crisp for at least two days — if the pie lasts that long."

¾ cup sugar
⅓ cup all-purpose flour
¼ teaspoon salt
2 cups milk
2 eggs, beaten
⅔ cup semisweet chocolate
    chips
1 tablespoon butter or
    margarine

1 teaspoon vanilla extract
2 large bananas
1 9-inch Butter Pecan Pie
    Crust (see below)
Whipped cream
Additional chocolate chips
    (optional)

In a medium saucepan, stir sugar, flour and salt. Gradually stir in milk until mixture is smooth. Over medium heat, cook and stir until mixture boils and boil for 2 minutes. Gradually stir about one-third of the hot mixture into the eggs, then stir back into hot mixture in saucepan. Stirring, bring to a boil and boil for 1 minute. Remove from heat. Stir in chocolate chips, butter or margarine, and vanilla until chocolate is melted. Slice bananas into cooled crust. Pour chocolate mixture over top. Chill at least 2 hours or overnight. Just before serving, garnish with whipped cream and chocolate chips. Makes 6 to 8 servings.

BUTTER PECAN PIE CRUST

1 cup all-purpose flour
¼ cup powdered sugar
⅛ teaspoon salt
6 tablespoons cold butter or
    margarine, cut in pieces

¼ cup finely chopped pecans
3 tablespoons ice water

In a medium bowl, stir flour, sugar and salt. With a pastry blender or two knives, cut in butter or margarine until mixture resembles coarse crumbs. Stir in pecans. Sprinkle water over the top and toss with a fork until uniformly moistened. Press dough firmly into a ball. Wrap in plastic wrap and chill in freezer for 20 minutes.

On a lightly floured surface, roll dough to ⅛-inch thickness and fit loosely into a 9-inch pie plate; flute edge. Place in freezer for 15 minutes. Meanwhile, preheat oven to 425°. Remove pie plate from freezer and prick bottom of shell. Bake for 15 minutes or until edges are lightly browned. Cover edges with foil and bake 5 to 10 minutes longer or until center is lightly browned. Cool on a wire rack. Makes 1 (9-inch) pastry shell.

Terry L. Ryan
Tecumseh, KS

PEANUT BUTTER CREAM PIE

"This cream pie is a Southern specialty, and the recipe is frequently requested by my friends who have tasted it. I especially like this pie since it can be made early in the day."

¾ cup powdered sugar	1 teaspoon vanilla extract
⅓ cup peanut butter	3 egg whites, at room
¾ cup sugar	temperature
⅓ cup all-purpose flour	¼ teaspoon cream of tartar
¼ teaspoon salt	6 tablespoons sugar
2 cups milk	1 baked 9-inch pie shell
3 egg yolks, lightly beaten	¼ cup chopped peanuts
2 tablespoons butter	

Preheat oven to 425°. In a small bowl, place powdered sugar. With a pastry blender or two knives, cut in peanut butter until mixture resembles coarse crumbs; set aside.

In a 2-quart saucepan, mix ¾ cup sugar, flour and salt. Stir in milk until smooth. Stirring over medium heat, bring to a boil and boil until thickened. Remove from heat. Gradually stir about one-third of the mixture into the egg yolks, then stir back into hot mixture in saucepan. Cook and stir over low heat 2 minutes longer (do not boil). Remove from heat. Stir in butter and ½ teaspoon of the vanilla. Cover; set aside.

In a small mixer bowl at high speed, beat egg whites, remaining ½ teaspoon vanilla and cream of tartar until soft peaks form. Gradually beat in 6 tablespoons sugar and continue beating until stiff and glossy.

Spread half of the peanut butter mixture in pie shell. Pour in hot filling and smooth top. Sprinkle remaining peanut butter mixture over filling to within ½ inch of outer edge. Spread meringue over filling, sealing to edge of pastry. Sprinkle peanuts on top. Bake for 8 to 10 minutes or until golden brown. Cool away from drafts for 3 hours before serving. Best eaten same day. Makes 6 to 8 servings.

Barbara Hamilton
Richmond, KY

COFFEE-PECAN MARSHMALLOW PIE

"Chocolate lovers, melt your favorite chocolate into this recipe. A six-ounce candy bar is yummy!"

½ cup coarsely chopped	1 cup whipping cream,
pecans	whipped
26 large marshmallows	1 ready-made graham
½ cup double-strength coffee	cracker crumb pie crust
1 teaspoon vanilla extract	

continued on next page . . .

Coffee-Pecan Marshmallow Pie continued . . .

Preheat oven to 400°. Spread pecans in a shallow pan. Bake for 5 minutes or until nuts are lightly toasted; set aside.

In a medium saucepan over low heat, melt marshmallows in coffee. Chill until slightly thickened. Whisk mixture if not smooth. Stir in nuts and vanilla. Fold in whipped cream. Spread in crust. Chill at least 1 hour before serving. Makes 6 servings.

Bobbie Reynolds
El Cajon, CA

RHUBARB-CRANBERRY PIE

"If I'm not running road races or marathons, you'll find me in the kitchen cooking. I love to try new recipes. This one is original. I just had some frozen cranberries and wanted to put something with the rhubarb to give it a different flavor."

4 cups sliced fresh rhubarb or frozen sliced rhubarb, thawed and drained	⅛ teaspoon salt
1 cup halved cranberries	6 drops red food color (optional)
1½ cups sugar	Pastry for a 9-inch double-crust pie
3 tablespoons quick-cooking tapioca	2 tablespoons butter or margarine
½ teaspoon ground cinnamon	1 egg, beaten (optional)

In a large bowl, mix rhubarb, cranberries, sugar, tapioca, cinnamon and salt; let stand for 15 minutes. Add food color.

Preheat oven to 425°. Divide dough almost in half. On a lightly floured surface, roll larger portion of dough to ⅛-inch thickness. Fit loosely into a 9-inch pie plate. Spread fruit mixture in pastry shell. Dot with butter or margarine.

Roll remaining dough for top crust and place over filling.* Trim both crusts ½ inch beyond rim of pie plate. Fold edges under; seal and flute. Cut a decorative design in center of pie to permit steam to escape.

For a browner crust, brush top of pie with egg. Bake for 10 minutes. Reduce heat to 375°. Bake 35 to 40 minutes longer or until rhubarb is tender when pierced with a fork. Cool on a wire rack. Serve slightly warm with vanilla ice cream if desired. Makes 8 servings.

*If desired, cut rolled dough into ½-inch strips. Weave strips in lattice fashion over filling, leaving 1 inch spaces between strips. Trim lattice strips even with bottom pastry. Fold bottom pastry over lattice strips; seal and flute.

Robin L. Robinson
Concord, NH

HUNGARIAN KIFFLES

(pictured on page 75)

"These delicate pastries are served at Christmastime. The recipe has been in my father's family for generations. They are very rich, but you can't eat just one."

- 2 packages (8 oz. each) cream cheese, softened
- 2 cups butter or margarine, softened
- 4 cups all-purpose flour
- Prune filling and/or thick apricot or raspberry preserves (about 1½ cups)
- Powdered sugar

In a large mixer bowl at medium speed, beat cream cheese and butter or margarine until creamy. At low speed, gradually beat in flour until moistened and begins to form a ball. Shape into forty-eight balls, about 2 tablespoons of dough each. Place balls in bowl, cover and chill at least 4 hours or overnight.

Preheat oven to 375°. On a lightly floured surface, roll each ball into a 4-inch circle. Place a rounded teaspoonful of filling or preserves in center of each; fold, forming a crescent, and press edges together with tines of a fork. Place on an ungreased baking sheet. Bake for 12 to 15 minutes or until golden brown. Cool on wire racks. Dredge in powdered sugar. Just before serving, sprinkle with powdered sugar. Store loosely covered in a cool dry place. Makes 4 dozen.

Denise A. Quillen
Lawton, OK

FROZEN PUMPKIN PIE

- 1 cup canned pumpkin
- ½ cup packed brown sugar
- ½ teaspoon ground cinnamon
- ½ teaspoon ground ginger
- ¼ teaspoon ground nutmeg
- ¼ teaspoon salt
- 1 quart vanilla ice cream, softened
- 1 ready-made graham cracker crumb pie crust
- Whipped cream
- Chopped nuts

In a small bowl, stir pumpkin, brown sugar, cinnamon, ginger, nutmeg and salt until blended; set aside.

In a large bowl, stir ice cream with a wooden spoon until smooth but not melted. Quickly stir pumpkin mixture into ice cream until blended. Immediately pour into pie crust. Cover and freeze at least 3 hours or until firm. Remove from freezer, uncover and let stand for 20 minutes before serving. Garnish with whipped cream and sprinkle with nuts just before serving. Makes 6 to 8 servings.

Vickie Rae Becker
Freeborn, MN

RAISIN TARTS

Pastry for a double-crust
   pie
1 cup raisins
½ cup coarsely chopped nuts
½ cup milk
2 eggs

1 cup packed brown sugar
2 tablespoons butter or
   margarine, melted
1 teaspoon vanilla extract
¼ teaspoon salt

Preheat oven to 400°. Divide pastry in half. On a lightly floured surface, roll one portion of dough at a time to ⅛-inch thickness. Cut six circles from each portion, about 4 inches each to fit inside 2½-inch muffin-pan cups. Fit pastry into cups, do not prick. Evenly distribute raisins and nuts in each tart shell.

In a medium bowl, whisk together milk and eggs. Add brown sugar, butter or margarine, vanilla and salt. Stir until blended. Pour evenly over raisins and nuts. Bake for 20 to 25 minutes or until pastry is golden and a pointed knife inserted in center comes out clean. Cool pans on a wire rack for 10 minutes, then carefully remove tarts from pan. Cool. Serve at room temperature. Refrigerate leftovers. Makes 12.

Diane Dobis
Mt. Morris, MI

HARVEST PIE

3 cups peeled and ¼-inch
   sliced tart apples (such as
   McIntosh or Granny Smith)
2 cups peeled and ¼-inch
   sliced pears
1 cup whole cranberries,
   cleaned
¼ cup raisins
1 unbaked 9-inch pie shell
   with high fluted edge

1 cup sugar
2 tablespoons all-purpose
   flour
½ teaspoon ground cinnamon
2 tablespoons butter or
   margarine, cut in ¼-inch
   pieces
½ cup walnut pieces
   Sweetened whipped cream
   or ice cream

Preheat oven to 400°. In a large bowl, combine apples, pears, cranberries and raisins. Transfer to pie shell.

In a small bowl, combine sugar, flour and cinnamon. Sprinkle over fruit. Dot with butter or margarine. Bake for 10 minutes. Reduce oven temperature to 350°; bake for 40 minutes. Top pie with walnuts and bake 15 minutes longer or until fruit is tender and crust is golden brown. Cool on a wire rack.

Serve at room temperature with whipped cream or ice cream. Makes 8 servings.

Susan Henry
Miami, FL

BLUEBERRY MERINGUE PIE

(pictured on page 75)

"I got the idea for this recipe from a very fine 'pie' restaurant here in California."

1 can (16½ oz.) blueberries
2 tablespoons cornstarch
1 cup sugar
3 egg yolks
1 cup dairy sour cream
1 teaspoon vanilla extract

1 8- or 9-inch baked pie shell
3 egg whites, at room
  temperature
⅛ teaspoon cream of tartar
6 tablespoons sugar

Preheat oven to 425°. Drain blueberries, reserving ¼ cup liquid. Set blueberries aside. In a small bowl, stir cornstarch and reserved liquid until smooth; set aside.

In a medium saucepan, stir 1 cup sugar and egg yolks until blended. Cook and stir constantly over low heat until mixture starts to bubble. Stir cornstarch mixture and add to saucepan. Stir in sour cream and blueberries. Increase heat to medium. Cook and stir until mixture boils and boil for 1 to 2 minutes or until thickened. Remove from heat. Stir in vanilla. Pour into pie shell.

In a small mixer bowl at high speed, beat egg whites and cream of tartar until soft peaks form. Gradually add 6 tablespoons sugar, beating until stiff and glossy. Spread meringue over filling, sealing to edge of pastry. Bake for 8 to 10 minutes or until golden brown. Cool to room temperature on a wire rack. Refrigerate for 2 hours before serving. Best served the same day. Makes 6 to 8 servings.

Violet Derderian
Van Nuys, CA

FROZEN CREAM LIME PIE

3 egg yolks, lightly beaten
½ cup sugar
2 to 3 teaspoons grated lime
  rind
¼ cup fresh lime juice
  Dash of salt
3 egg whites
5 drops green food color

1 cup whipping cream
1 ready-made graham
  cracker crumb pie crust
  Whipped topping
  Fresh lime slices
  Chopped pistachio nuts
  (optional)

In a medium saucepan, mix egg yolks, ¼ cup of the sugar, lime rind and juice, and salt until blended. Stirring constantly over medium-low heat, cook until thickened and mixture coats a spoon. Chill.

continued on next page . . .

Frozen Cream Lime Pie continued . . .

In a small mixer bowl at high speed, beat egg whites until soft peaks form. Gradually beat in remaining ¼ cup sugar and continue beating until stiff and glossy. Stir one-fourth of the egg whites and food color into egg yolk mixture to lighten. Fold in remaining whites. In small mixer bowl at medium speed, beat cream until stiff peaks form. Fold into egg white mixture until blended. Pour into crumb crust. Freeze at least 4 hours or until firm. When frozen, cover with foil. Remove from freezer, uncover and let stand for 20 minutes before serving. Garnish with whipped topping, lime slices and nuts just before serving. Makes 6 to 8 servings.

FROZEN CREAM LIME DESSERT: Pour mixture into a 1-quart serving bowl instead of crumb crust. Freeze and garnish as above.

Mrs. J. Bognich
Omaha, NE

ITALIAN MINI-CREAM PUFFS

1 cup water	4 large eggs
½ cup margarine	Ricotta Filling (see below)
1 cup all-purpose flour	Powdered sugar

Preheat oven to 400°. In a medium saucepan over medium heat, bring water and margarine to a rolling boil; reduce heat to low. Add flour all at once and stir vigorously with a wire whisk or wooden spoon until mixture forms a ball. Remove from heat. Add eggs, one at a time, beating well after each addition until mixture is smooth. Drop dough, 1 teaspoon at a time, about 1½ inches apart onto ungreased baking sheets. Bake for 22 to 25 minutes or until golden brown. Remove from baking sheets; cool on wire racks. Store in an airtight container in a cool place.

To serve, cut tops from puffs and fill each with about 1 tablespoon of filling. Lightly dust tops with powdered sugar. Makes 60 to 70.

RICOTTA FILLING

24 ounces ricotta cheese	⅔ cup chopped mixed
½ to ⅔ cup sugar	candied fruit (optional)
½ teaspoon vanilla extract	
1 cup semisweet chocolate mini chips	

In a small mixer bowl at medium speed, beat ricotta cheese, sugar and vanilla for 30 seconds or until smooth. At low speed, beat in mini chips and candied fruit. Cover and chill if making ahead. Use as filling for cream puffs. Makes about 4½ cups.

Angela M. Leuthardt
Bolingbrook, IL

MACAROON-TOP APPLE PIE

4 cups peeled, sliced tart
   cooking apples
1 cup sugar
¼ teaspoon ground cinnamon
2 tablespoons butter or
   margarine, softened

1 egg
½ cup all-purpose flour
½ teaspoon baking powder
¼ teaspoon salt
½ cup flaked coconut
½ teaspoon vanilla extract

Preheat oven to 375°. Place apples in a 9-inch pie plate. In a small bowl, mix ½ cup of the sugar and cinnamon; sprinkle over apples. Bake for 20 minutes.

Meanwhile, in a small mixer bowl at medium speed, beat remaining ½ cup sugar and butter or margarine until fluffy. Beat in egg until well mixed. At low speed, beat in flour, baking powder and salt until blended. Stir in coconut and vanilla. Spread over hot apples to within 1 inch of edge of pie plate. Bake 30 minutes longer or until apples are tender and top is browned.

Serve hot or at room temperature with sweetened whipped cream or vanilla ice cream if desired. Makes 6 servings.

Eileen C. Hart
Avon, CT

Eileen C. Hart

LEMON SOUR CREAM TARTS

(pictured on page 75)

1 cup sugar
3 tablespoons cornstarch
1¼ cups milk
1 tablespoon grated lemon
   rind
⅓ cup lemon juice
¼ cup margarine

3 egg yolks, lightly beaten
1 cup dairy sour cream
8 baked tart shells (about
   3½ × 1½ inches each)
Non-dairy whipped topping
   (optional)
Small purple gumdrops

In a medium saucepan, mix sugar and cornstarch. Stir in milk, lemon rind and juice until sugar is dissolved. Add margarine. Stirring over medium heat, bring to a boil and boil for 1 to 2 minutes or until thickened. Remove from heat.

Gradually stir about one-third of the hot mixture into the egg yolks, then stir back into hot mixture in saucepan. Cook and stir over low heat 2 minutes longer. Cool slightly. Stir in sour cream until well blended. Transfer to a bowl, cover and chill.

Fill tart shells up to 1 hour before serving. Garnish with whipped topping and gumdrops cut into flower shapes with lemon rind centers. Refrigerate leftovers. Makes 8.

Rebecca S. Clark
Manchester, MO

Rebecca S. Clark

Desserts and Sweets

BUTTER PECAN CRUNCH ICE CREAM

"My mother-in-law developed this recipe for vanilla ice cream, and I created the additions to make the butter pecan version. Now we make it in Colorado where we moved to enjoy the mountains and participate in the winter sports, hiking and backpacking."

6 eggs	1 quart milk
3¼ cups packed brown sugar	6 tablespoons butter
1 tablespoon vanilla extract	1½ cups chopped pecans
Dash of salt	1 package (6 oz.) almond
1 quart whipping cream	brickle chips (optional)

In a large mixer bowl at medium speed, beat eggs until frothy. At low speed, gradually beat in 2½ cups of the brown sugar. At medium speed, add vanilla and salt and beat for 3 minutes or until brown sugar is almost dissolved. Add cream and beat until sugar is dissolved. Pour into a chilled 5-quart ice cream freezer container; stir in milk. Pack and churn according to manufacturer's directions.

Meanwhile, in a 10-inch skillet over low heat, melt butter. Add pecans and cook, stirring frequently, for 10 minutes or until pecans are browned. Sprinkle remaining ¾ cup brown sugar over nuts. Cook, stirring constantly, for 3 to 4 minutes or just until brown sugar begins to melt. Spread on several layers of paper towels to cool.

Five minutes before freezing is complete, add sugared nuts and almond brickle chips to mixture and continue churning until frozen as hard as you wish. Makes about 1 gallon.

Sharon Setliff
Broomfield, CO

Doris Setliff
Mathis, TX

Pictured on the preceding page, top to bottom, are Pumpkin Pudding Squares (see page 88), Holiday Cream Dessert (see page 90), and Raspberry Mousse Meringues (see page 89).

BROWNIE CONCOCTION

"I had day-old brownies on hand and did not want to waste them, so I just experimented and this is the result. It came out quite good."

1 recipe brownies baked in a 13 × 9 × 2-inch pan, cooled	Milk for pudding (about 3 cups)
¼ cup brandy or almond liqueur	1 cup whipping cream, whipped
2 packages (10 oz. each) frozen raspberries, thawed and drained	½ cup toasted slivered almonds
1 package (5¼ oz.) chocolate pudding and pie filling mix	

Crumble brownies and spread in the same baking pan. Sprinkle with brandy or liqueur. Top with raspberries.

Prepare pudding according to package directions; cool for 5 minutes. Spread over raspberries. Chill for 20 minutes. Spread whipped cream over pudding and sprinkle with almonds. Chill at least 2 hours before serving. Makes 15 servings.

Helga Smith
Liberty Hill, TX

RHUBARB SQUARES

"This recipe has been in the family for many, many years and loved by all."

2½ cups all-purpose flour	4 cups thinly sliced fresh rhubarb or frozen sliced rhubarb, thawed and drained
¾ cup powdered sugar	
1 cup butter or margarine	
2 cups sugar	
4 eggs, lightly beaten	Vanilla ice cream or whipped cream (optional)
1 teaspoon salt	

Preheat oven to 350°. Grease a 13 × 9 × 2-inch baking pan. In a large bowl, mix 2 cups of the flour and powdered sugar. With a pastry blender or two knives, cut butter or margarine into flour and sugar until mixture resembles fine crumbs. Press evenly into bottom of pan; bake for 20 minutes or until golden brown. Cool on a wire rack for 5 minutes.

In a large bowl, mix sugar, remaining ½ cup flour, eggs and salt until well blended. Stir in rhubarb. Pour evenly over crust. Bake for 45 minutes or until set. Loosen edges with a sharp knife while still warm. Cool pan on a wire rack at least 30 minutes. Cut into squares. Serve warm with ice cream or whipped cream. Refrigerate any leftovers. Makes 15 servings.

Barbara Smith
Grimes, IA

PUMPKIN PUDDING SQUARES

(pictured on page 85)

"My family likes this better than pumpkin pie! We enjoy it year round . . . it's an easy company dessert which can be served warm or cold. Real whipped cream is best!"

1 can (29 oz.) pumpkin	1 teaspoon vanilla extract
2½ cups evaporated milk	½ teaspoon ground nutmeg
2 cups sugar	½ teaspoon ground cinnamon
1 cup all-purpose flour	¼ teaspoon baking soda
½ cup butter or margarine, melted	¼ teaspoon salt
	Whipped cream
3 eggs, lightly beaten	

Preheat oven to 450°. Grease a 13×9×2-inch baking pan. In a large mixer bowl at medium speed, beat pumpkin, evaporated milk, sugar, flour, butter or margarine, eggs, vanilla, nutmeg, cinnamon, baking soda and salt for 1 minute or until smooth and well blended. Pour into pan. Bake for 30 to 35 minutes or until a wooden pick inserted in center comes out clean. Cut in squares and serve warm or cold with whipped cream. Makes 12 (3 inches each).

Mrs. Billie L. Taylor
Afton, VA

LEMON ICEBOX DESSERT

"I have had this recipe for about 20 years. It has been enjoyed at coffee and dessert evenings, church suppers, etc."

6 egg whites, at room temperature	6 egg yolks
¼ teaspoon salt	3 tablespoons grated lemon rind
¼ teaspoon cream of tartar	½ cup lemon juice
¼ teaspoon white vinegar	2 cups whipping cream
3 cups sugar	1 cup chopped walnuts
1 teaspoon vanilla extract	

Preheat oven to 300°. Butter a 15½×10½×1-inch jelly roll pan. In a large mixer bowl at high speed, beat egg whites until frothy. Add salt, cream of tartar and vinegar; beat until soft peaks form. Gradually beat in 2 cups of the sugar and continue beating until stiff and glossy. Beat in vanilla. Spread evenly in pan. Bake for 1 hour. Cool completely on a wire rack.

Meanwhile, in a heavy 3-quart saucepan over low heat, mix egg yolks, remaining 1 cup sugar, lemon rind and juice. Stirring constantly over low heat, cook for 10 minutes or until thickened. Cool completely.

continued on next page . . .

Lemon Icebox Dessert continued . . .

In a small mixer bowl at medium speed, beat cream until soft peaks form. Spread half of the whipped cream over meringue. Carefully spread lemon mixture over cream, top with remaining cream and sprinkle with walnuts. Chill, uncovered, for 24 hours before serving. Makes 15 servings.

Constance M. Ellway
Hailey, ID

RASPBERRY MOUSSE MERINGUES

(pictured on page 85)

"I serve this dessert on individual silver plates to top off an elegant dinner or when I want to do something special for after-dinner guests. Of my many hobbies, collecting recipes and cooking are my favorites."

4 egg whites, at room temperature	1 package (10 oz.) frozen raspberries, thawed (reserve 6 berries for garnish)
¼ teaspoon salt	
⅛ teaspoon cream of tartar	1 envelope unflavored gelatin
1½ cups sugar	
⅓ cup finely chopped almonds	½ cup almond liqueur
	1 cup whipping cream, whipped

Preheat oven to 275°. Line a baking sheet with brown paper. In a large mixer bowl at high speed, beat egg whites until frothy. Add salt and cream of tartar; beat until stiff. Beat in sugar, 1 tablespoon at a time, and continue beating for about 8 minutes or until very stiff and glossy. Spoon six mounds of the mixture onto brown paper, about 2 inches apart. Shape each into a 2½-inch circle with an indentation in the center. Sprinkle almonds in center of each. Bake for 40 minutes. Turn off oven and without opening oven door, cool completely, about 4 hours. If making ahead, cover loosely and store in a cool place.

Place berries and juice in a blender container or food processor bowl; cover. Blend or process until puréed. Press mixture through a sieve with a rubber scraper to remove seeds. In a 2-quart saucepan, mix purée and gelatin; let stand for 1 minute. Cook and stir over low heat until gelatin is dissolved. Remove from heat. Stir in liqueur. Chill until thickened and syrupy. Fold in whipped cream. Chill until mixture mounds when dropped from a spoon. Spoon into center of each meringue. Garnish tops with reserved berries. Chill at least 30 minutes or until filling is firm. Serve on individual dessert plates. Makes 6 servings.

Kathryn B. Delaney
Golden Valley, MN

GONE WITH THE WIND DESSERT

"Our family likes it plain — without the bananas, but I use sliced bananas as a garnish with quartered maraschino cherries in a flower design."

1 envelope unflavored gelatin	3 tablespoons sugar
½ cup cold water	3 tablespoons butter or margarine, melted
2 egg yolks	2 egg whites
1 cup sugar	1 cup whipping cream, whipped
1 cup milk	
1 teaspoon vanilla extract	2 medium bananas, sliced (optional)
1½ cups graham cracker crumbs	

In a small bowl, sprinkle gelatin over water; let stand for 1 minute; set aside.

In a 1-quart saucepan, beat egg yolks well. Stir in 1 cup sugar and milk. Stirring constantly over medium heat, bring to a boil and boil for 2 minutes. Remove from heat. Add gelatin mixture and vanilla; stir until gelatin is dissolved. Pour into a large bowl; cover and chill for 1 hour or until mixture mounds when dropped from a spoon.

In a small bowl, mix graham cracker crumbs, 3 tablespoons sugar and butter or margarine. Reserve ⅓ cup for topping. Pat remaining crumb mixture into a 2-quart oblong baking dish.

In a small mixer bowl at high speed, beat egg whites until stiff but not dry. Fold whipped cream then egg whites into custard. Fold in bananas. Pour into dish, sprinkle with reserved crumb mixture. Chill for 3 hours or until set. Makes 18 servings.

Jeanette Willis
Logan, UT

HOLIDAY CREAM DESSERT

(pictured on page 85)

"Originally the recipe was an experiment, but has been so successful that it is now a family favorite. There are so many variations. I serve it with blueberries and raspberries for the 4th of July and add green food color for St. Patrick's Day."

1 envelope unflavored gelatin	1 teaspoon vanilla extract
¾ cup cold water	1 package (10 oz.) frozen red raspberries, thawed and warmed, or sliced, sweetened strawberries
¾ cup sugar	
1 cup whipping cream	
1 cup dairy sour cream	

continued on next page . . .

Holiday Cream Dessert continued . . .

In a 2-quart saucepan, sprinkle gelatin over cold water. Let stand for 1 minute. Add sugar. Cook and stir over low heat for 5 minutes or until sugar and gelatin are dissolved. Stir in whipping cream. Chill for about 1 hour or until mixture is the consistency of raw egg whites. Stir in sour cream and vanilla until smooth. Pour into six custard cups or dessert dishes. Chill until set.

To serve, top with berries and juice. Makes 6 servings.

Note: To make a larger quantity in a mold as shown on page 85, double the recipe and use 3 envelopes gelatin. The molded dessert will be firmer than the individual servings.

Pat Rossitto
Santa Ana, CA

PEACH SUPREME

"This is very much like a custard with peaches added and topped with an almond-flavored topping . . . one of my favorite flavors."

1 can (29 oz.) peach halves, well drained	½ cup almond paste (½ of 8 oz. can), at room temperature, crumbled
3 eggs	
1½ cups milk	⅓ cup sugar
¼ cup sugar	⅓ cup butter or margarine, softened
1 teaspoon vanilla extract	
Pinch of salt	Boiling water
½ cup all-purpose flour	¼ cup flaked coconut
	Whipped cream

Preheat oven to 325°. Place nine peach halves, rounded-side up, in an 8×8×2-inch baking dish; set aside. If any peach halves are left, reserve for another use.

In a medium bowl, beat eggs well. Add milk, ¼ cup sugar, vanilla and salt, stirring until well blended and sugar is dissolved. Carefully pour mixture around peaches.

In the same bowl using the back of a spoon or your fingers, mix flour, almond paste, ⅓ cup sugar and butter or margarine until well blended. Divide dough into nine portions (about 2 tablespoons each) and flatten slightly into rounds, about 2½ inches in diameter. Place one on top of each peach half (edges will go into liquid). Set baking dish in a larger pan (13×9×2-inch) and place in oven. Fill larger pan with boiling water to a depth of 1 inch. Bake for 50 minutes; sprinkle top with coconut. Bake 5 minutes longer or until a knife inserted in custard comes out clean. Carefully remove baking dish from water; cool on a wire rack.

Cut into squares and serve warm or at room temperature with whipped cream if desired. Makes 9 servings.

Betty Harvey
Albuquerque, NM

CAJUN BREAD PUDDING

"I come from a large family, full of love, and with lots of good food in the kitchen. The women in my family are all good cooks and start everything from scratch. We have always cooked for a dozen or more. I love to please my family and friends with 'tender loving care' that I usually conjure up in my kitchen."

4 eggs	1 cup shredded coconut
3 cups chopped pecans	6 tablespoons butter or
3 cups milk	margarine, melted
1 can (15¼ oz.) crushed	3 tablespoons vanilla extract
pineapple in its own juice	10 cups crumbled day-old
1 can (14 oz.) sweetened	French bread
condensed milk	Brandy Sauce (see below)
1 cup raisins	

Preheat oven to 375°. Butter an 8×8×2-inch and a 13×9×2-inch baking pan. In a large bowl, lightly beat eggs. Add pecans, milk, pineapple with juice, condensed milk, raisins, coconut, butter or margarine, and vanilla; mix well. Add bread and mix just until bread is moistened. Spoon evenly into baking pans. Bake for 50 to 60 minutes or until brown and a knife inserted in center comes out clean.

Serve warm with Brandy Sauce. Makes 24 (½-cup) servings.

BRANDY SAUCE

2 cups powdered sugar	1 egg yolk
1 cup butter, softened	1 cup brandy

In a 2-quart saucepan over medium heat, stir powdered sugar and butter until blended. Add egg yolk. Stirring constantly, bring to just under a boil. Gradually stir in brandy. Cool to room temperature. (Sauce will thicken as it cools.) Serve over warm Cajun Bread Pudding. Refrigerate any leftovers. Makes about 3 cups.

Mary Brady Arendt
Waggaman, LA

RECIPE INDEX

*Recipes photographed

93